The Silk Road

An Enthralling Overview of the Ancient Trade Routes That Connected China to Europe

© Copyright 2024 - All rights reserved.

The content contained within this book may not be reproduced, duplicated, or transmitted without direct written permission from the author or the publisher.

Under no circumstances will any blame or legal responsibility be held against the publisher, or author, for any damages, reparation, or monetary loss due to the information contained within this book, either directly or indirectly.

Legal Notice:

This book is copyright protected. It is only for personal use. You cannot amend, distribute, sell, use, quote, or paraphrase any part, or the content within this book, without the consent of the author or publisher.

Disclaimer Notice:

Please note the information contained within this document is for educational and entertainment purposes only. All effort has been executed to present accurate, up-to-date, reliable, and complete information. No warranties of any kind are declared or implied. Readers acknowledge that the author is not engaging in the rendering of legal, financial, medical, or professional advice. The content within this book has been derived from various sources. Please consult a licensed professional before attempting any techniques outlined in this book.

By reading this document, the reader agrees that under no circumstances is the author responsible for any losses, direct or indirect, that are incurred as a result of the use of the information contained within this document, including, but not limited to, errors, omissions, or inaccuracies.

Free limited time bonus

Stop for a moment. We have a free bonus set up for you. The problem is this: we forget 90% of everything that we read after 7 days. Crazy fact, right? Here's the solution: we've created a printable, 1-page pdf summary for this book that you're reading now. All you have to do to get your free pdf summary is to go to the following website:

https://livetolearn.lpages.co/enthrallinghistory/

Once you do, it will be intuitive. Enjoy, and thank you!

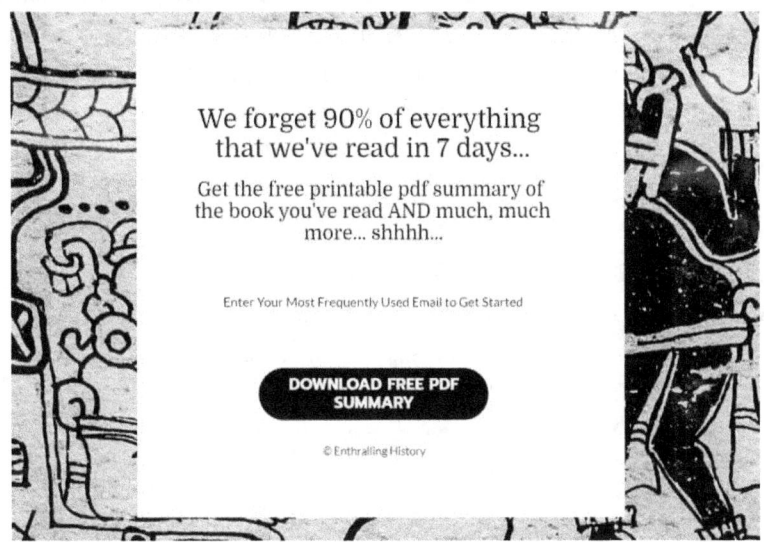

Table of Contents

INTRODUCTION 1
CHAPTER 1: THE SILK ROAD: A JOURNEY THROUGH TIME 3
CHAPTER 2: THE ORIGINS OF THE SILK ROAD..11
CHAPTER 3: THE GREAT EMPIRES OF THE SILK ROAD 19
CHAPTER 4: THE SILK ROAD'S MOST VALUABLE GOODS.....................31
CHAPTER 5: THE TRAVELERS OF THE SILK ROAD...................................43
CHAPTER 6: THE SILK ROAD: ART AND ARCHITECTURE 51
CHAPTER 7: RELIGION AND THE SILK ROAD..63
CHAPTER 8: THE SILK ROAD: SCIENCE AND TECHNOLOGY 72
CHAPTER 9: THE SILK LEGACY..79
CONCLUSION..87
HERE'S ANOTHER BOOK BY ENTHRALLING HISTORY THAT
YOU MIGHT LIKE..91
FREE LIMITED TIME BONUS..92
BIBLIOGRAPHY 93

Introduction

Living in a world with the instant connectivity of the internet and the speed of modern travel makes it sometimes difficult to imagine what life was like thousands of years ago when the world was limited to what a person could reach by horseback near their home.

Not only was a person's travel limited, but their access to things like food, fabrics, and other supplies was restricted to whatever grew near them or what was created by people in their village. There was not a lot of variety in goods, and even the knowledge and religion that people experienced were limited since they rarely had the opportunity to come in contact with different cultures.

The Silk Road changed this way of life for multiple cultures all along the four-thousand-mile east-to-west trade route. Tradesmen carried goods, although far more than goods were spread from east to west and, in return, from west to east.

People in the West tasted tropical fruits from the East for the first time. The trade in spices revolutionized cooking around the globe. Religions spread from one region to the next. Scientific advancements began to happen as cultures put their ideas and resources together.

The Silk Road brought together pastoral and agrarian societies, uniting very different cultures from all over Eurasia and beyond with the trade of goods and the sharing of ideas.

The Silk Road also made many empires wealthy, thanks to the sale of goods and the taxes paid on items at ports of entry. Western empires and kingdoms lusted over luxury goods from the Far East, like silk and gemstones. Stories of journeys to exotic places along the Silk Road fueled imaginations for centuries and led to famous literary works.

What were the historical factors that inspired humans to trade with each other, though?

This book will break it down for you in simple terms. See how it began from the earliest points in history. Watch the rise and fall of the Silk Road alongside the rise and fall of empires. Find out who traveled the Silk Road and why, and gain insight into the fascinating impact the Silk Road had on everything in the world, from architecture to cooking.

What would life be like today if humanity had never begun trading along the Silk Road?

Chapter 1: The Silk Road: A Journey Through Time

Imagine a road that extends four thousand miles, spreads between three continents, and winds through some of the most intense and harrowing landscapes on Earth.

From the Yellow Sea in the east to the Mediterranean Sea in the west, the Silk Road was a network of pathways rather than a single road. These pathways connected the edges of Europe to East Asia, bringing together many cultures and societies that were vastly different from each other.

Travelers followed these trade routes through the Gobi Desert, where temperature extremes and the lack of water challenged caravans and where shifting sand threatened both humans and their goods. The Silk Road twisted through the freezing Himalayan Mountains, where brave travelers suffered from altitude sickness, bitter cold, and deadly avalanches, and traversed the grassy plains of the Eurasian Steppe.

Every turn of the Silk Road came with the possibility of death by nature or attack by roving bandits. In a time before planes, trains, and automobiles and in the days before vast sea trade routes were well established, the main source of transportation was horseback or camel caravan. The journey along the Silk Road was slow and arduous for travelers.

The Silk Road connected the countries and regions of China, central Asia, Persia (modern-day Iran), the Middle East, India, parts of East Africa, and the edges of Europe. The Mediterranean Sea was an important hub along the Silk Road, connecting the countries in Asia to Europe in the west. Major cities like the Egyptian city of Alexandria became trade hubs. Other important connecting cities were Constantinople, which is known today as Istanbul, and Antioch in Syria, which was a Greek city during the Hellenistic period.

The paths of the Silk Road were first worn smooth by the feet of people who carried goods for sale and trade. However, the Silk Road quickly became more than just a place where goods were transported. Along with the silks, spices, and dyes came the exchange of ideas, religions, art, traditions, and technologies as travelers interacted with different cultures and religions.

Cultural diffusion had almost as big of an impact on world history as the exchange of goods. In fact, the Silk Road's impact on world history was so powerful that it will be forever known as a bridge between civilizations and a testament to the strength of human collaboration across diverse cultures and long distances.

Despite being named the Silk Road in our modern history books, it was not actually a paved road or even a designated pathway in most areas. No one living along the Silk Road called it by this name. Instead, they would refer to it as the road to the next village or the road to a certain landmark up ahead. The unmarked paths of the Silk Road were made up of mountain passes, rivers, and deserts, and directions were given from one oasis or village to the next. Most people hired local guides to get them through each section of the road safely.

The Silk Road did not earn its official historical name until a German geographer by the name of Baron Ferdinand von Richthofen coined the phrase "the Silk Road" in 1877 when he used it in his atlas.

The Silk Road's popularity as a trade route spanned almost a millennium! It began in the 2nd century BCE and slowly faded away around the 15th century CE.

Let us take a quick look at the timeline of the Silk Road as its significance and use ebbed and flowed throughout various regions and throughout world history. With just a glance, you can see how the Silk Road was woven into many famous historical events and well-known time periods.

2nd Century BCE

What could have possibly motivated people to leave home and venture out on a dangerous journey along the Silk Road? To understand their motivations, we need to consider what life was like in the 2nd century BCE.

When the Silk Road was first becoming established, the Han dynasty ruled over China. The Chinese people were agrarian, which means they were farmers who cultivated the land. In the 2nd century BCE, China made the world-altering decision to more aggressively pursue trade with other people besides the nomads and nearby civilizations in central Asia.

Central Asia was populated with numerous tribes at this time. Chinese Emperor Wu Di sent out an exploratory mission to visit some of these tribes in an effort to officially establish trade. He sent his envoy Zhang Qian on the first journey along what would become known as the Silk Road. Zhang Qian's journey was filled with unexpected twists and turns, as he was captured by nomads and spent ten years in captivity before escaping and continuing on.

In the end, his journey was not only successful, but it also remains well known today since it significantly contributed to Chinese history. Zhang Qian gathered information about different cultures, regions, and routes and reported back to Emperor Wu Di, empowering him to make the necessary diplomatic connections in order to pave the way for friendly trade. This led to the development of the Silk Road and earned Zhang Qian the nickname "Father of the Silk Road."

1st to 2nd Century CE

The Roman Empire blazed onto the scene of history during the 1st century BCE. As you may know, the Roman Empire was powerful and ever expanding. The Romans also loved silk, and they developed an enjoyment of many other items from the Far East, including spices, gemstones, clothing, precious metals, and ivory. Fur, chemicals for curing leather, and paper were also popular trade items. Regular patterns of trade between the Roman Empire and the Far East began to solidify along the Silk Road during this time period.

The Roman Empire and the eastern Asian countries were so far apart that a single person could not travel the entire route alone. Trade was facilitated by a series of middlemen from tribes and regions all along the Silk Road. With these intermediaries, the sharing of cultural influences between regions began.

Want to know a lesser-known fact about the Silk Road? Silk was one of the many goods transported along the trade route, but arguably one of the most essential items was paper! Paper was invented in the East in the

1st century CE, although it would take a few centuries before it became a popular trade item on the Silk Road.

The earliest evidence of paper ever discovered is in the form of a written report addressed to Han Emperor Ho-di. It is dated to 105 CE.[1] From there, paper spread along the earliest routes of the Silk Road through China. Papers dating back to the 2nd century CE have been found in the cities of Loulan, Kotan, Kusha, and Dunhuang.

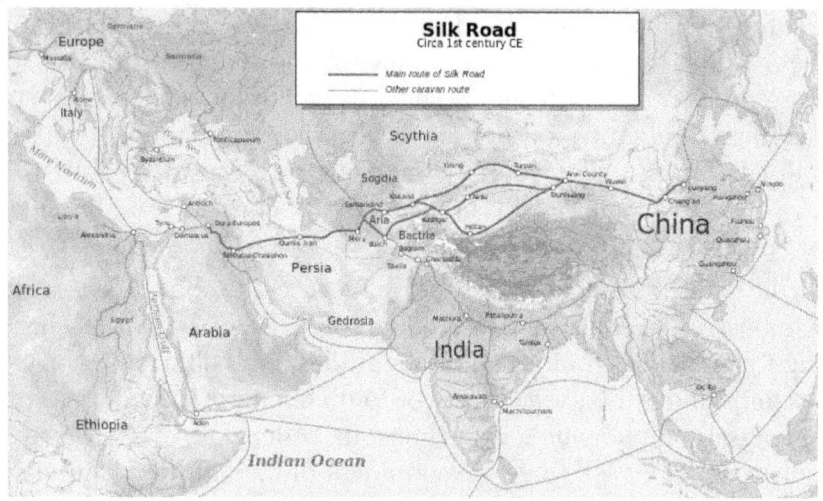

The Silk Road in the 1st century CE.
Kaidor, CC BY-SA 4.0 <https://creativecommons.org/licenses/by-sa/4.0>, via Wikimedia Commons; https://commons.wikimedia.org/wiki/File:Silk_Road_in_the_I_century_AD_-_en.svg

4th to 5th Centuries CE

The world roared right along into the 4th century CE. The paths of the Silk Road were becoming well traveled by this point in time; well, that is until a hiccup occurred. When the Western Roman Empire faced collapse, the demand for luxury items from the Far East plummeted.

6th to 7th Centuries CE

Nevertheless, the Silk Road stayed busy. The Byzantine Empire continued to grow in importance during the 6th century CE, and it established itself as an essential intermediary in the trade between the East and the West along the Silk Road, sharing its culture and art along with its merchandise.

---

[1] http://www.silk-road.com/artl/papermaking.shtml/

7th to 8th Centuries CE

The Chinese Tang dynasty peaked in the East during this period. At the same time, the Islamic caliphates were busy making all kinds of connections, further adding to the Silk Road and turning it into a web of pathways. The Silk Road was now large enough to connect the Mediterranean cities, central Asia, and China.

13th Century CE

Fast forward in time. Everything had been humming along quite smoothly. Trade along the Silk Road for the last few centuries had been magnificent. In fact, trade continued to build relationships between groups of people who would otherwise have nothing in common.

During the 13th century, a ruthless player in history rose to power and established his territory over a large part of the Silk Road. You may have heard of him before. His name was Genghis Khan of the Mongol Empire. He was followed by another famous Mongolian name in history, Kublai Khan.

The Mongol Empire held control over a key part of the Silk Road, linking China to the Mediterranean Sea.[2] Though the Mongols were known for their military conquests and fierce battle strategies, the Mongol Empire was also responsible for a key peace called the Pax Mongolica, which lasted from the 13th to the 14th century. The Pax Mongolica brought peace between different cultures and territories along the Silk Road, allowing trade to flourish because of the safety and stability that could be found in the region.

The Mongols also developed a type of postal system called the Yam. This helped information and trade goods move along the routes of the Silk Road and through all Mongolian territories more easily and efficiently, providing excellent opportunities for growth, both economically and in their administration.

Although the Mongols are often remembered as brutal warriors, many of their leaders had diplomatic tendencies and promoted cultural tolerance. For instance, Kublai Khan was interested in academia and the arts. He encouraged the translation of books and writings so they could be shared with different cultures along the Silk Road.

---

[2] https://en.unesco.org/silkroad/content/did-you-know-silk-routes-mongols

He also sponsored scholars in their studies and education. Thanks to Kublai Khan, ancient knowledge that had been nearly lost was once again appreciated and preserved, and that information was spread alongside trade on the Silk Road. Records show over twenty thousand public schools were put in place during his time as emperor, which helped elevate the people of the region to become a better educated society.[a]

Another well-known person began his epic journey along the Silk Road during this same time period: Marco Polo.

Marco Polo served as a foreign emissary to Kublai Khan from 1215 to 1294, during which time he collected knowledge of the region, including Mongolian customs and inventions.

Although historians still debate whether Marco Polo ever traveled east, the writings about Marco Polo's journeys to the Far East introduced Europeans to the magic and wonder of lands they had never really imagined before. This fascination fueled the West to have more interest in trade with the East.

An illustration of Marco Polo's caravan to the East.
https://commons.wikimedia.org/wiki/File:Caravane_sur_la_Route_de_la_soie_-_Atlas_catalan.jpg

---

[a] https://courses.lumenlearning.com/suny-hccc-worldcivilization/chapter/kublai-khan/

14th to 15th Centuries CE

The times changed quickly during the period between the 14th and 15th centuries. The great Mongol Empire began to wane, with regional states developing in its place. These regional states were powerful. They blocked parts of the Silk Road, hindering the flow of goods and making travel more dangerous.

History produced another familiar name during this time, a very famous traveler along the Silk Road: the Black Death.

Due to the incubation period of the plague, the Silk Road was able to assist in the spread of the Black Death, as well as cultural exchange and exotic goods. People would pick up the illness in one area but not show any symptoms. Then, when they arrived at their next stop, they would fall ill and share their germs along a new area of the trade route. As you may imagine, the resulting panic and death caused trade to slow.

In addition to the Black Death, the fall of Constantinople during this same time period also contributed to the slowdown in trade along the Silk Road. Constantinople was the capital of the Byzantine Empire. The city connected the Eastern and Western trade routes, making it a vital hub for travelers looking to trade goods along both land and sea routes.

In 1453, the city was conquered by the Ottoman Turks, immediately causing a change in the flow of trade items due to new taxes and potential restrictions on goods that were allowed to be transported through the region. Constantinople was still a vibrant economic center under the Ottoman Empire; however, the higher tax rate was a major deterrent to the Silk Road trade. Trade links were severed, with the Ottoman Empire becoming the new middleman for trade with the East. This change in power caused a loss in stability for regular traders who were used to Byzantine-controlled Constantinople.[4]

The Age of Exploration was just beginning in Europe, and it was partially spurred on by the need to find a new trade route that did not include the fallen Constantinople. This led to the discovery of a maritime route that went around the tip of Africa, making long and cumbersome journeys over treacherous terrain a thing of the past for many eager tradesmen and further contributing to the decline of the Silk Road's land-based trade routes.

---

[4] https://www.tutorchase.com/answers/ib/history/what-economic-impacts-followed-the-fall-of-constantinople

16th to 18th Centuries CE

Welcome to the Age of Exploration! During this time, brave explorers sailed the ocean blue in search of shortcuts and new maritime trade routes to connect the East and the West.

Of course, you have likely heard of Christopher Columbus, but have you ever read about the Portuguese explorer Vasco da Gama? He sailed around the southernmost tip of Africa, Cape Hope, and reached the continent of India. This was a significant development in the world of trade. Europeans had traveled to India in boats for the first time, completely skipping over the land-based Silk Road trade paths.

Let us not forget to mention the Ottoman Empire. During the 16th to the 18th century, it was in control of important areas along the Silk Road, including the aforementioned city of Constantinople.

The Ottoman Empire also controlled Anatolia, a region that contained multiple trade routes, connecting the Ottoman Empire to central Asia, the Middle East, and Europe. The Ottomans actually controlled a very large swath of territory that included vital cities like Damascus, Aleppo, Baghdad, Beirut, and Jerusalem. They also held power over territories in North Africa, which was not a part of the overland trade routes but held important ports for maritime trade.

19th Century CE

The Silk Road became obsolete at this point in history. Colonies were the new popular thing for countries to establish, which meant ships were sailing all around the world. Instead of meandering along a treacherous landscape, people were now sailing directly to their trade destination, cutting out the need for a middleman and, along with it, ending the need for the ancient network of Silk Road pathways.

Now that you have gotten a broad overview of the Silk Road's timeline throughout history, let us take a deep dive into the factors that went behind the birth of the Silk Road. How did people trade before the Silk Road? Why did China wish to establish trade with the West?

Hop on your camel or a Tibetan horse if you prefer, and take a ride as we go way back to the Steppe Route and the Tea Horse Road.

Chapter 2: The Origins of the Silk Road

The Steppe Route

The very beginnings of trade pathways in China can be attributed to two routes: the Steppe Route and the Tea Horse Road.

The Steppe Route was an ancient trade route linking China with the Middle East, central Asia, and eventually the Mediterranean region.

Where exactly was the Steppe Route, though? Today, the route is occupied by the countries of Kazakhstan, northern Mongolia, the southern regions of Russia along the Caspian Sea and the Volga River, the southern parts of Ukraine, the Crimean Peninsula, areas of Turkmenistan along the Caspian Sea, and Uzbekistan.

The terrain was flat, open grassland in central Asia and eastern Europe. The soil and climate were not suitable for growing crops, but grass grew there in abundance. This grassy area went on for many miles and was home to nomadic tribes herding livestock. The flat terrain made travel easy for tradesmen traveling in caravans of horses and camels.

The Eurasian Steppe Route was dissected by rougher areas, such as the Ural Mountains, the Altai Mountains, the Sayan Mountains, and the Greater Khingan range.

When looking at our timeline for the Silk Road, we have to consider where to place the beginnings of the Steppe Route. It was around long before the Silk Road became established in history; in fact, it was around before our timeline even began.

The Steppe Route has no formal beginning. It started in antiquity, as far back as humans have been living in central Asia. Scholars estimate the Steppe Route began in the 4th millennium BCE, possibly around the Bronze Age.

It is important to note a world-altering invention that showed up in central Asia during the Bronze Age: the spoked wheel. Wheeled transport undoubtedly played a role in the beginnings of long-distance trade. As wagons and chariots were developed, people discovered they could move goods over longer distances. With those goods, people came into contact with different cultures, and the sharing of ideas began.

The Steppe Route grew alongside the rise of Inner Eurasian pastoralism.[5] These would be the first farmers of the Steppe, the people who practiced animal husbandry. Unsurprisingly, the first trade routes followed the paths made by nomadic livestock herders.

Initially, nomadic people were hesitant to travel and trade. As their groups grew larger, more resources were needed, fueling the need to explore further. As people explored, they came into contact with different tribes and cultures. Theft became an issue, which prompted nomads to build fences for their livestock and design defenses for their tribes. People banded together in cultural communities to support each other.

As weather patterns changed, the nomads were forced to move from place to place to find better grazing land. This was a key factor in the early development of trade routes. Nomads were forced to come into contact with each other whether they liked it or not.

Soon, trade between civilizations and nomadic tribes became frequent along the Steppe Route as people shared goods between cultures. Few people traveled the full length of the trade route, though. Instead, middlemen and intermediaries were used to pass goods throughout the region of central Asia and into the Middle East (they would be similar to couriers).

Scholars estimate that the Steppe Route was in use at least two thousand years prior to the Silk Road.[6]

---

[5] Christian, David. "Silk Roads or Steppe Roads?" https://www.jstor.org/stable/20078816.
[6] Torr, Geordie. *The Silk Roads: A History of the Great Trading Routes Between East and West.*

As the years passed, the route gradually expanded until it reached the Mediterranean Sea. The original Steppe Route is now known as the Northern Silk Road.

Travelers along the route exchanged silk and other textiles. Gemstones, such as turquoise, lapis lazuli, agate, and nephrite, were just some of the riches exchanged between regions. Ceramics, spices, and precious metals were exchanged too.

Travel contributed to the spread of Buddhism from India into central Asia and China. Politically, the riches made from trade helped to grow the powerful Persian Empire, the Parthian Empire, and eventually the Islamic caliphates.

The Steppe Route was the main artery that formed the blueprint for the Silk Road and set the stage for what would become the most historically significant trade route in history. Early political diplomacy and the new linguistic connections that formed over time were essential elements that helped form the future of the Silk Road.

The Tea Horse Road

The Tea Horse Road was another early artery of the Silk Road. Ancient Chinese records refer to *Chamadao*, which translates to "the tea and horse road."

The Tea Horse Road was precisely what its name described. That is to say, it was a road primarily established for the trade of two things: Chinese tea leaves and Tibetan horses.

The Chinese in the 1st century CE were a military society. Horses were exceedingly valuable for moving men from place to place and for riding into battle. Horses also played an essential role in moving people and goods along dangerous and tedious trade routes.

Imagine the ultimate battle horse, one with all of the most powerful features: extreme endurance, surefootedness over rocky mountainous terrain, a body unfazed by the high altitudes of the region, fur and skin that could withstand wild winds and biting snow, and the physical strength to survive off of very little food in remote areas without access to grazing pastures. Basically, this super horse could eat three blades of grass and charge fearlessly into a wintery battle scene on a rocky slope.

For other people, instead of charging into battle, this super horse would fearlessly navigate along narrow pathways and through harsh weather along trade routes.

The Chinese were in luck because neighboring Tibet just so happened to breed horses that met this exact description.

The rough terrain of Himalayan Tibet was a unique environment to breed horses. As a result of the high altitude and rocky slopes, Tibetan horses evolved to become perfect creatures for perilous trade routes. They could make it over mountains and through blizzards and the shifting sands of the desert.

A Tibetan horse was also associated with a high social status, similar to the fast foreign sports cars of today. This made them a hot trade item.

You may laugh when you think of the Chinese offering to trade some tea leaves for a powerful, well-bred horse. The Tibetans, however? They were not laughing. They were pleased to make the trade.

The importance of tea leaves was paramount in Chinese and Tibetan societies. They provided medicinal benefits. Tea was associated with hospitality, friendship, and gatherings, especially along the Silk Road. Sophisticated families could offer tea to Silk Road travelers. Tea provided an assuage for the senses with its smell, taste, and even rich colors. In some areas, tea leaves could even be used as currency.[7]

Not every region along the Silk Road could grow tea due to the harsh climates, which further upped the allure of tea leaves as a trade item.

And for the Chinese? Tea leaves were lightweight and easy to transport. They took up little space when stored in bricks that weighed between 0.45 kilograms and 2.75 kilograms.[8] The tea leaves also sold at a high price.

The Chinese and Tibetans began traveling up and down the Tea Horse Road between China and Tibet, establishing an essential trade route that would later become known as the Southern Silk Road or the Southwest Silk Road. This road was one of the most prominent parts of the webbed pathways making up the Silk Road.

The Han Dynasty

Perhaps the most important early contributor to the Silk Road was the Han dynasty (206 BCE–220 CE). The Han dynasty decided to start

---

[7] "Ancient Tea and Horse Caravan Road." http://www.silkroadfoundation.org/newsletter/2004vol2num1/tea.htm.

[8] "Ancient Tea Horse Road." https://www.bbc.com/travel/article/20120830-asias-ancient-tea-horse-road.

formally making trade agreements with the areas around them and then with regions that were farther away.

In 138 BCE, Emperor Wu Di of the Han dynasty decided he wanted to send a court official to make contact with the Yuezhi, one of their traditional allies. The emperor learned that the Yuezhi were being threatened by the Han dynasty's common enemy, the Xiongnu.

To reach the Yuezhi, whoever volunteered to go would need to pass west through territory controlled by the Xiongnu. Only one person was brave enough to take the journey: a petty court official named Zhang Qian.

He set out with a party of one hundred men. Unluckily for Zhang Qian, he was captured by the Xiongnu. They held him captive for ten years, forcing him to move with the imperial party as they traveled around the Steppe. During that time, he married a Xiongnu woman and had several children.

Zhang Qian made his way to the Yuezhi kingdom but was unsuccessful in making a treaty with them. He stayed for a year before attempting the journey home to report back to the emperor.

Zhang Qian was captured by the Xiongnu a second time, but he managed to escape with his wife and children during a disturbance in the Xiongnu camp. Zhang Qian was away for thirteen years in total.

Upon his release, he continued traveling around central Asia, where he explored the wealthy civilizations that had flourished under Alexander the Great. These Hellenistic Greek cities had arts and culture that Zhang had never seen before. He reported back to the emperor that the cities were heavily fortified with walls, towers, and gates. He also told the emperor about all the wonders he had witnessed, which unfortunately were not recorded in detail for us to read in the present day.

We can guess what he saw from what we know about Hellenistic cities, though. The cities were laid out in grids using organized urban planning. They featured public buildings like libraries, gyms, and bathhouses. They were famous for their theaters, amphitheaters, and stone walkways.

Most importantly, Zhang Qian visited markets in each city, where he saw goods that he had never seen before.

The emperor was intrigued, so he sent Zhang Qian back out on the road to explore further. Thankfully, the diplomat was not held prisoner on this trip. Instead, he made his way to Persia, where he discovered a new breed of horses in what is present-day Uzbekistan. These were known as the Ferghana horse, and they were said to be so powerful that they sweat blood.

Scientists have now made an educated guess that the bloody sweat was likely drops of blood from biting parasites. A little less impressive, on the whole, but in ancient times, it seemed pretty amazing. The people believed these powerful horses were the result of interbreeding mortal and heavenly horses.

Emperor Wudi wanted to hear more about the horses. He even wanted some for himself. Zhang Qian also told him of amazing glassware and of a new type of bamboo he had never seen before. There was also an unusual cloth they were selling, which was reported to have come from India, a place completely unknown to the Han dynasty.

Zhang Qian is now historically known as the "Father of the Silk Road," which seems like a title he certainly earned with his determination and perseverance.

The biggest question we might be asking about the Han dynasty is why. Why did the emperor decide to pursue trade outside of his local region?

Curiosity about unknown places like India and new exotic goods was definitely a strong motivator. But was that enough inspiration to send more men out on perilous journeys? Remember, this was a period fraught with warring tribes and unfriendly civilizations. The only way to establish diplomatic relationships with other people groups and cultures was to ride up on a horse and say hello, which could be somewhat risky if the diplomat was not a welcome visitor. (See Zhang Qian's experiences and failed treaty attempt!)

Yet, the Han dynasty still pursued the idea of establishing trade far from home. What were its other reasons beyond curiosity?

The Han dynasty's first reason was a selfish one. If the Han dynasty wanted to expand beyond its borders, it could either start a battle and claim territory or gradually spread its influence through diplomacy and trade with neighboring states. Instead of choosing violence, the Han dynasty chose to be peaceful. It formed treaties with its neighbors to prevent any conflicts and established solid trade agreements that were mutually beneficial for both parties.

The Han dynasty intelligently used trade to foster alliances, which allowed it a buffer from contentious relationships with other regions, especially the Xiongnu Confederation to its north. These alliances made the empire more secure and far less vulnerable to sudden attacks or takeovers. The Han dynasty now had friends in its corner, ready to stand together if needed because everyone was benefiting from the trade of goods and the sharing of ideas.

Sneakily, the Han dynasty also began to establish something known as protectorates. Of course, if trade routes were to be established, they had to be safe and secure, right?

When the trade routes extended outside of the Han dynasty's region and snaked through dangerous territory, someone had to be in charge to keep the peace and safety of the tradesmen. How were they going to protect the traded goods from theft?

While setting up these protected routes, the Han dynasty had the opportunity to exert its influence over the government in these regions, further expanding its power by sticking its fingers in its neighbor's governments.

As the officially established trade routes grew, the Han dynasty began to reap the economic benefits of reliable, organized trade. The emperor decided to invest in the military. The Han traded for powerful Ferghana horses and grew their cavalry. They fought off the nomads and began building their own fortified walls, which would later be part of the Great Wall of China.

The wall served as a defense, naturally, but it had another use. Travelers were forced to pay a tax to the emperor on the goods they were carrying. This added to the wealth of the Han dynasty. There were only a few gates in the Great Wall for travelers to pass through. These quickly became centers of trade along the Silk Road. Soon, there were inns for weary travelers, markets to trade goods, and restaurants. These ports of entry also began to serve as border patrol and customs locations for the empire.

Next, the Han dynasty invested in its own administration, growing its government. The Han started making scientific advancements, too! It is amazing what a steady cash flow can do. Suddenly, the Han dynasty was measuring time with water clocks and inventing paper to write on. Paper exploded in popularity and eventually became a heavily traded item along the Silk Road.

Paper was especially important to the spread of Buddhism. Scripture was written down and easily transported along the earliest routes of the Silk Road. Paper allowed scripture and teachings to be translated into various languages and dialects and to be saved for academic study. Buddhism spread like wildfire with the support of Chinese leaders, but we will talk more about that later.

While physical goods were being traded, something even more powerful was happening intangibly. The Han dynasty was asserting what is known as soft power over those it interacted with on the trade route.

Soft power refers to the influence of a nation over other people. The Han dynasty was sharing its values, ideas, philosophies, and culture without using force. It was happening naturally as people from the Han dynasty interacted with others along the trade route. By sharing their music, art, fashion, and food, they were able to create a sense of unity between different cultures, strengthening their alliances and securing their position on the world trade stage.

The foundations for the Silk Road were officially laid in place by the diplomatic pursuits of the Han dynasty. A physical road was not built, but the network of treaties, alliances, and protectorates created by the Han dynasty set the stage for the east-to-west sharing of both goods and cultures to take off and explode into a superhighway. Wealthy empires waited at either end of the Silk Road, clamoring for luxury items from the opposite end of the trade route.

The emergence of the Silk Road is still a topic of study among anthropologists, archaeologists, and historians today. Archaeological discoveries at the Eurasian Steppe along the Steppe Route have forced historians to rethink what they thought they knew about life in the 2nd century BCE. Gravesites and tombs reveal grave goods that are from a different culture than the deceased, proving that trade was booming earlier than previously thought.

DNA testing and grave detecting from satellites are two of the modern tools now available to archaeologists that have put a new spin on the emergence of the Silk Road. The story is still changing as we learn new facts with each excavation.

Chapter 3: The Great Empires of the Silk Road

Arguably, one of the most fascinating things about looking back at history with clear hindsight is the ability to view the rise and fall of empires across the globe. The Silk Road is particularly fascinating in that it served as a thread to knit together empires and clearly contributed to both the rise and, at times, the fall of great and powerful empires.

The four main empires that thrived along the Silk Road were the Persian Empire, the Hellenistic Parthian Empire, the Roman Empire, and the Tang dynasty.

The Persian Empire (550 BCE–330 BCE)

The Persian Empire at its greatest extent in 500 BCE.
Cattette, CC BY 4.0 <https://creativecommons.org/licenses/by/4.0>, via Wikimedia Commons; https://commons.wikimedia.org/wiki/File:Achaemenid_Empire_500_BCE.jpg

You may have heard of the famous Persian Empire referenced in history and stories. Even if you are not familiar with the details, chances are you know of some of Persia's most famous wares. For example, have you ever seen a Persian rug?

The Persian Empire was also known as the Achaemenid Empire. It was famous for rock carvings and metalwork, among many other things. It was also the first civilization to develop a postal service using its Royal Road.

The Persian Empire stretched from regions of Iran to Iraq, across Egypt and Turkey, and into central Asia. The central location of Persia gave the empire control over essential parts of the earliest predecessor to the Silk Road: the Royal Road. The Persian Empire's famous Royal Road was an ancient highway that ran from the eastern city of Susa to the western city of Sardis, crossing most of the Persian Empire. The Royal Road would become an integral piece of the trade route and laid a major part of the foundation for the larger Silk Road network.

Unlike the Silk Road's treacherous web of trade route paths, the Royal Road was designed for ease of travel. Its purpose was quick communication and efficient transportation from city to city. The Royal Road had multiple relay stations, where couriers waited to carry messages from one point to the next, making communication across the empire a speedy affair in the days before emails or text messages. The Royal Road also provided the administration with a way to communicate effectively across many miles. The Royal Road allowed the Persian army to march quickly across all sections of the large empire, keeping Persia strong and secure.

The Silk Road was never intended to move men and messages across a vast empire like the Royal Road. However, as time went on, the trade routes became more consolidated under the Mongol Empire. It was at this time the Silk Road intersected with the Royal Road at multiple points, adding another layer of depth to the strength and vitality of the Silk Road trade network and making the historical Royal Road one of the most important channels of the Silk Road.

Susa, in today's modern Iran, was possibly the most important city on the intersecting routes. Due to its geographical location, Susa was one of the key points between the East and the West. Goods traded there included textiles, silks, dyes, spices, dried fruits, nuts, grains, herbs, precious metals, metalwork such as tools, magnificent gemstones, pottery, ceramics, paper, books, and manuscripts with knowledge of other cultures and religions.

Another important city along the two routes was Ctesiphon. This city is now modern-day Baghdad, Iraq. The Tigris River runs through this region. Ctesiphon was known for both the trade of goods and diplomatic interactions between cities, states, and empires since so many travelers passed through the area.

Persepolis was the capital of the Persian Empire. It was not directly linked to the Silk Road, but it was a main stop along the Royal Road, as it was the empire's hub of political administration and power. It is worth mentioning this city since it played such a vital role in trade and diplomatic interactions along the route.

The Royal Road ended in Sardis, which is in modern-day Turkey. After Sardis, the Silk Road continued to connect to other regions through maritime trade routes across the Mediterranean Sea, making Sardis a key location for cultural exchange.

There is one intangible thing that the Persian Empire used its Silk Road connections to spread. It was a religion, but it was not the Islamic religion that has become almost synonymous with the Middle East today.

The Persian Empire's religion was called Zoroastrianism. This was a monotheistic religion, meaning they believed in a single god. It was named after the Persian prophet Zoroaster, also known as Zarathustra. Zoroaster broke out of the typical belief systems held by other Indo-Iranian groups who worshiped multiple deities. Thanks in part to the Silk Road, his monotheistic belief system began to spread like wildfire. Many scholars agree that Zoroastrianism is the world's first monotheistic faith.

What is the name of Zoroastrianism's single god? It is Ahura Mazda, at least according to a vision Zoroaster had when he was thirty years old. Its temples were known as fire temples, places of worship containing an altar and an eternal flame.

You may now be asking what Zoroastrianism has to do with the Silk Road.

Well, as mentioned, Zoroaster's messages spread along the Silk Road with traded goods. It is possible that the tenets of Zoroastrianism helped influence bits and pieces of the three major Abrahamic religions: Judaism, Christianity, and Islam.

For example, word about Zoroastrianism reached the Kingdom of Judea, where the Jewish people were living in captivity. The major ideas of Zoroastrianism are a single god, heaven, hell, and a day of judgment. Does this sound familiar to anyone else?

Imagine for just a moment the impact Abrahamic religions have had on the world throughout history.

As Zoroastrianism spread along the Silk Road, it laid the foundation for the basis of religions that would contribute to many things, both positive and negative. Countless famous works of art have been based on monotheistic religions. How many institutions of higher learning have been based on these religions? In the Middle Ages, the religious medieval European, Middle Eastern, and African universities played a crucial role in spreading knowledge far and wide.

Common morals were established between cultures and countries, with a monotheistic religion as the common denominator. These morals contributed to the basis of laws and constitutions used by governments across the world. Colonies were created, wars were waged, and people groups were oppressed and conquered all in the name of a monotheistic religion.

Without Zoroastrianism spreading along the Silk Road, the worldview for many countries and cultures throughout history and even today would likely look very different.

Eventually, the great Persian Empire outgrew its britches. The empire expanded along the eastern shore of the Mediterranean, and the Persians thought they could add Greek colonies to the empire. However, this backfired somewhat since the colonies, which were located along the edge of modern-day Turkey, were not very excited to become Persian.

When the Greek colonies rebelled, they were given support by mainland Greek city-states, effectively starting a war between Persia and Greece that would ultimately end in the downfall of the Persian Empire.

The Parthian Empire (247 BCE–224 CE)

As the Persian Empire declined, the next great civilization to rise up on the timeline of history was the Parthian Empire.

You may be familiar with the famous Hellenistic period. This period occurred alongside the Parthian Empire on our timeline. The Parthian Empire was located farther to the east, where it took in some Hellenistic influences from neighbors traveling along the Silk Road.

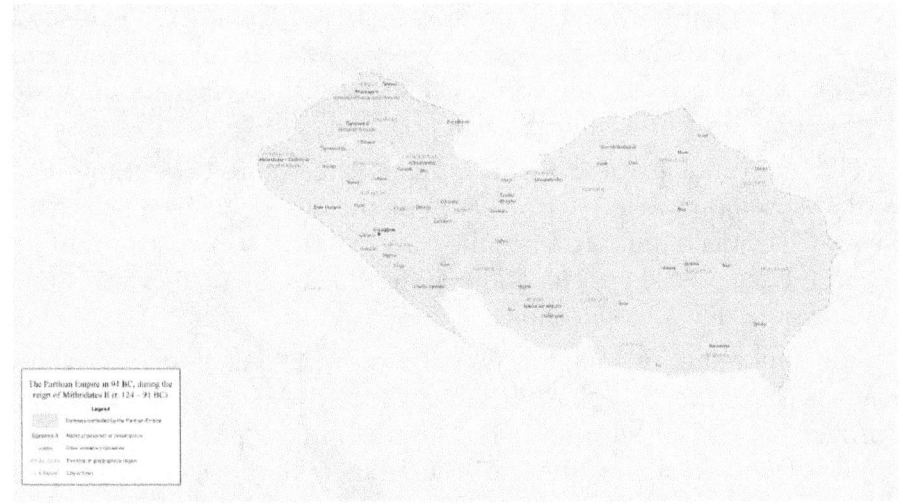

The Parthian Empire at its greatest extent in 94 BCE.
Original file by Ro4444, edited by me, CC BY-SA 4.0 <https://creativecommons.org/licenses/by-sa/4.0>, via Wikimedia Commons
https://commons.wikimedia.org/wiki/File:Map_of_the_Parthian_Empire_under_Mithridates_II.svg

The heart of the Parthian Empire was located in modern-day Iran. To the east, the empire covered what is today parts of Turkey, Armenia, and Turkmenistan. The empire spread outward from Iran north to the Caspian Sea. In the south, it went all the way to the Persian Gulf. Like many empires, the borders of the Parthian Empire changed throughout its history.

The position of the Parthian Empire along the Silk Road allowed the empire to control overland trade between the Mediterranean and Asia. The capture of key cities on the Persian Gulf gave the Parthian Empire control over vital commercial centers for maritime trade.

As a power play, the Parthians used their mighty military and their geographical position to gatekeep the silk trade. They refused to allow the Romans to trade directly with the Chinese Han dynasty, which had the coveted silk. The Parthians kept themselves planted firmly in the center as middlemen between the Han and Rome.

The *Hou Hanshu* (*Book of the Later Han*) is a well-known historical account of the Han dynasty written by Fan Ye, who lived from 398 to 445 CE. This quote from the *Hou Hanshu* explains what the Han discovered about Parthia's gatekeeping of the silk trade along the Silk Road.

"They [the Romans] trade with Anxi [Parthia] and Tianzhu [Northwest India] by sea. The profit margin is ten to one. The king of this country always wanted to send envoys to Han, but Anxi, wishing to control the trade in multi-colored Chinese silks, blocked the route to prevent [the Romans] getting through [to China]."[9]

The government of the Parthian Empire recognized how important Parthia's position was as intermediaries on the Silk Road. The politicians enjoyed the wealth, and in turn, they prioritized a strong army and an organized state to keep everything along their part of the Silk Road running smoothly without conflict.

The importance of trade was so well recognized that, despite tensions, conflicts between the Han dynasty, the Roman Empire, and the Parthians were resolved peacefully. During this time period, the Roman emperor sent a letter to the Parthian ruler asking that they form an alliance with each other based on their trade of spices and textiles. The deal was successfully agreed upon.

Diplomacy was the goal of all three empires. The development of positive relations between empires through the tenets of diplomacy was just another world-changing tally mark on the list of concepts heavily influenced by the existence of the Silk Road. People realized the mutual success of economies through commercial trade, even between countries and empires that had tensions with each other, was more important than fighting.

The Roman Republic (509-27 BCE) and The Roman Empire (27 BCE-476 CE)

Unlike other empires we have discussed, the Roman Republic and the Roman Empire did not directly use the Silk Road as a main trade route. The Roman use of the Silk Road was rather indirect, going through intermediaries like the Parthians to make contact with the Far East.

In the year 53 BCE, the Romans suffered what is known as one of their worst military defeats. Marcus Licinius Crassus and his men were defeated by the Parthian Empire at the Battle of Carrhae.

The battle raged throughout the morning hours, with waves of Parthian men attacking the Roman troops repeatedly. The Romans held

---

[9] Fan Ye. *Hou Hanshu* (*Book of the Later Han*).

strong and did not waver, hoping they would still be able to defeat the Parthians and win the battle.

It was just after noon when something completely unexpected occurred. The Parthians staged another round of attacks, this time with a twist. The Parthian soldiers came running into battle, banging on drums, shooting arrows, and making a cacophony of noise. As the Roman soldiers looked on in shock, the Parthians unfurled bright, shimmering silk banners.

Roman Historian Lucius Annaeus Florus, who lived from 74 to 130 CE, gives a description of the silk banners.

"And so he [Crassus] had scarcely reached Carrhae when the king's generals, Silaces and Surenus, displayed all around him their standards, uttering with gold and silken pennons; then without delay the cavalry, pouring around on all sides, showered their weapons as thick as hail or rain upon them. Thus, the army was destroyed in lamentable slaughter."[10]

No one is certain if the silk banners were opened to rally the Parthian troops or if the Parthians actually meant to shock the Romans, but in any case, the Romans stood with their mouths agape.

They had never before seen silk. The bold colors, the brilliant way the material reflected the light on the battlefield, and the beauty of the textile stunned them. This moment's pause allowed the Parthians to gain the foothold they needed. The Roman soldiers began running in shock and breaking rank, giving the Parthians the advantage in battle.

Of course, the entire battle was not lost simply because the Romans saw the dazzling banners. Other factors were at play, namely some poor battle strategy decisions made by Crassus and the excellent military strategies used by the Parthians.

Some historians believe this fateful day was the first time the Roman Empire came in contact with silk. From then on, the Romans wanted to find a way to get silk for themselves. The door was opened to begin trading along the Silk Road to acquire this luxurious textile from the Chinese. Soon, the Roman elite were clamoring to get their hands on as much expensive silk as they could.

---

[10] https://archive.org/stream/in.ernet.dli.2015.184585/2015.184585.Lucius-Annaeus-Florus_djvu.txt

pg. 212.

For the Romans, silk was a mysterious textile. They had no knowledge of the silkworms the Chinese bred and used to create the beautiful cloth. Some thought it grew on trees. Others were suspicious that the love of silk would cause jealousy and immorality and make men want to own an excess of goods that would leave the empire weakened by selfishness.

The Roman obsession with silk did not die down. Instead, it grew into a mania until the Romans were trading silk and other luxury items through intermediaries as quickly as they could. Silk was incredibly expensive, comparable to pearls or purple dye, and was often striped with gold, further driving up the wow factor and the cost.

During the first two centuries of the Common Era, the Romans imported various other luxury goods alongside the silk threads. They purchased precious stones, such as pearls and emeralds, and spices. Indian and Arabic spices like nutmeg, cloves, cardamom, and pepper were some of the most popular spices that had double uses. Spices were not just for eating—they also served as aphrodisiacs to go along with the allure of the sensual silks.

Historians estimate the Romans were spending the present-day equivalent of up to one billion dollars USD on luxury imports per year by 65 CE!

In the 4th century CE, the Roman Empire promoted the tolerance of Christianity under Emperor Constantine, which led to many people converting to Christianity. Cities along trade routes suddenly became hubs of the religion. This had a lasting impact on the spread of Christianity along the Silk Road.

Missionaries also went out along the Silk Road to establish churches in the biggest trade and port cities. They used the tradesmen and intermediaries to spread the seeds of Christianity from west to east.

Throughout the long history of the Silk Road, the Romans and the Chinese both gained immense amounts of soft power through trade. They spread their cultural influences far and wide. The Chinese grew rich from the trade of silk, and the Romans gained economic benefits from sending their own goods to the Chinese, which included wine and brightly colored glass vases that became a prized luxury good in China.

A green Roman glass cup found in an Eastern Han tomb.
https://commons.wikimedia.org/wiki/File:Green_glass_Roman_cup_unearthed_at_Eastern_Han_tomb,_Guixian,_China.jpg

However, with all the mutual benefits the two empires shared, they did not meet face to face, only exchanging goods through many hands along the route between China and the Mediterranean.

How would history have been different if the Chinese and the Romans directly interacted with each other? We can guess, but we will never truly know the answer.

The Tang Dynasty (618-907 CE)

There is one major empire involved in the Silk Road trade that we have not yet mentioned: the Tang dynasty in China.

To give a clear picture of our timeline, the Tang dynasty existed alongside the rise of medieval European states and the beginning of the Middle Ages. India was also beginning its medieval period. In the Americas, the Maya civilization was collapsing, and the Post-Classic period was beginning. The Byzantine Empire and the Islamic caliphates were in conflict and also involved in trade along the Silk Road.

The world was becoming a busy place. As people began to explore more, trade and diplomacy were of the utmost importance on the world stage. The rulers of the Tang dynasty recognized the importance of trade for their empire. Infrastructure was very important to keep trade moving along smoothly throughout the region.

The Tang dynasty prided itself on organization and administration. They had around 32,100 kilometers (19,900 miles) of postal routes throughout the region, with mail carried by both horse and boat.[11]

The Tang dynasty preferred to move a large amount of goods within China by boat. The Chinese built their famous Grand Canal during the Sui dynasty (581-618 CE). During the Tang dynasty, the canal was expanded and meticulously maintained. The canal moved goods between the Yellow River and the Yangtze River, including grain that was taken as payment for taxes, agricultural products, and the military. The Grand Canal connected northern and southern China by boat.

The military transports along the canal allowed China to maintain a strong, secure country. Threats could be quickly extinguished, with troops and horses, along with their artillery, speeding down the canal at a moment's notice. Similar to the Silk Road, knowledge, culture, and ideas also traveled with the men who sailed down the canal and back. This helped China unify as a country, as the north and the south began sharing common ideals.

The Tang dynasty quickly took advantage of this efficient transportation route. They began charging a tax for merchants to transport goods along the Grand Canal, boosting its economy.

The Silk Road intersected with the Grand Canal at various port cities, which became multicultural hubs of trade. Yangzhou, Suzhou, and Hangzhou were a few of these hub cities. Merchants from the Silk Road gathered in these cities to trade goods.

One hub of international trade that is still famous in China today is the Tang West Market in Xi'an (then known as Chang'an).

Chang'an was an important city during the Tang dynasty that hosted the largest market in the world during that time period. Archaeological surveys show the market was about one square kilometer or 0.4 square miles. The market was divided into nine rectangular regions, similar to city blocks, with more than two hundred types of goods being traded in thousands of different stores. An estimated 150,000 people a day came through the market.

---

[11] "Trade under the Tang Dynasty." https://courses.lumenlearning.com/suny-hccc-worldcivilization/chapter/trade-under-the-tang-dynasty/.

The sellers were both local and international, with the goods heavily influenced by trade on the Silk Road. Chang'an became a center of cultural studies for people along the Silk Road, thanks to being a hub of trade and all of the friendly political diplomacy surrounding the Tang West Market. Many scholars from other regions longed to come to Chang'an to study.

The Silk Road and the Grand Canal were both instrumental in creating the Tang West Market and catapulting Chang'an into such a unique, multicultural municipality.

You have certainly heard of the famous Panama Canal. You may be surprised to learn that the Tang dynasty's Grand Canal is twenty-two times longer than the Panama Canal. The Panama Canal is only around fifty miles (eighty kilometers) in length. China's Grand Canal is 1,104 miles (1,776 kilometers) long! It was quite an engineering feat for the time period during which it was constructed.

The Grand Canal was constructed over a period of six years in order to connect the capital city of Beijing to the city of Hangzhou in the southern farming region of China. The Grand Canal was not an entirely new canal; rather, it was a project made to connect multiple existing canals across China.

For example, there was already a canal between the Yangtze River and the Huai River and another canal called the Hong Gou Canal that connected the Yellow River to the Bian River. These ancient canals grew into the Grand Canal under the strict leadership of Emperor Yang during the Sui dynasty, a short-lived dynasty that preceded the Tang dynasty.

Emperor Yang was known for his tyrannical ways, forcing many farmers to work themselves to death on the Grand Canal project. Although the exact number is not known, it took millions of Chinese men to construct the canal. The project was finally completed in 609 CE.

By the 1400s, the Grand Canal was bustling with activity. The Chinese government had over eleven thousand barges in use for transporting grain up and down the canal. During that period, there were more than forty-five thousand workers who maintained the canal on a regular basis.

While the citizens were busy constructing the Grand Canal and trading goods during the Tang dynasty, the administration was feverishly bustling around the Silk Road on many diplomatic missions. In fact, the Tang dynasty made friendly contact with more than three hundred different regions along the trade routes.[12]

The Tang dynasty presented a united China, drawing together smaller tribes and different regions with a more unified culture. The Tang dynasty was partly aided by the spread of information along the Grand Canal, resulting in strong national power. Ambassadors from the Tang dynasty were curious people and very adept at understanding new cultures or making intelligent assessments of new places. This gave these passionate ambassadors an advantage on the world stage, making them wildly successful and prosperous at peaceful trade along the Silk Road.

---

[12] "The Prosperity of the Silk Road in the Tang Dynasty." http://en.shaanxi.gov.cn/as/hac/hos/201704/t20170428_1595517.html.

Chapter 4: The Silk Road's Most Valuable Goods

Now that we know the major role played by the Silk Road in world history, perhaps we should discuss what was traded along the Silk Road. Of course, silk was the most famous item; after all, the route was named after it. While silk undoubtedly left an indescribable mark on world history, it was not the only important thing shared between countries and cultures along the Silk Road.

Silk

As legend has it, around the year 3000 BCE, Empress Leizu was having a cup of tea when a silkworm cocoon plopped down from the tree above right into her cup. Surprised, the empress pulled the cocoon out of her tea and began to unroll it. She admired the long, silky fibers and decided to try weaving some of them.

The result was magnificent. Her husband, the Yellow Emperor, recommended she study the life of the silkworm. She instructed her servants to help her begin cultivating silkworms, and it was then that Empress Leizu became famous in Chinese mythology as the goddess of silk.

This story is just a legend passed down through the generations. What has history actually uncovered about the beginnings of silk? Since silk is a delicate textile, it does not survive well in tombs or graves, but archaeologists have still been able to uncover quite a few clues about the origins of silk in human history.

More than 8,500 years ago, humanity was in the Neolithic Age or, as some prefer to call it, the New Stone Age. Humans had recently transitioned from hunting and gathering to cultivating crops and breeding livestock. They also created settled agricultural communities, which became the first villages. People had more time with their settled lifestyles, so they began to experiment with metalworking, spend more time on religion, and develop their artistic talents.

Pottery was a common art form during this period. Almost every artistic creation had a practical use. Bowls or jugs were decorated with scenes depicting daily life, religion, or intricate patterns but were used for cooking or storage.

Surprisingly, silk weaving was possibly one of the first arts practiced in Neolithic China. Archaeologists discovered the remnants of silk fibroin inside Neolithic tombs that were excavated in Jiahu, China.

While the exact date has not been pinpointed, these tombs were from the period between 7000 and 5000 BCE. Alongside the silk fibers, archaeologists discovered remnants of bone needles and weaving tools.

In nearby Shanxi, pieces of a cleanly cut silk cocoon were discovered while excavating a site left behind by the Yangshao culture. This suggests that between 4000 and 3000 BCE, humans were breeding silkworms. A solid white cocoon only comes from the domesticated silkworm.

At a Yangshao excavation site dated to 3630 BCE, a woven silk wrap was discovered shrouding the body of a child placed inside a burial urn. This is the earliest sample archaeologists have found of intact silk woven textiles.

For many years, China had a ban on the import of silkworms. Silkworm cultivation, or sericulture, was a closely guarded Chinese secret. It was so secretive that other cultures who enjoyed the trade of this gorgeous textile along the Silk Road began developing their own origin stories to explain how silk was produced. The Romans, for example, were convinced that silk came from special tree leaves.

Did you know that in China, sericulture and silk weaving was only for the richest in society? It was an art form mainly for women, and at first, it was restricted to only the imperial family. As time went on, silk was also allowed for noble women. It was not until the Qing dynasty (1644-1911) that everyday peasants were allowed access to silk.

During the Han dynasty, which was the origins of the official Silk Road on our timeline, silk became far more than just a textile. Silk was similar to gold in that it was used as payments to the government alongside bronze coins. Silk was shared with other powers when Chinese emperors sent out diplomatic missions to explore and establish trade across neighboring regions.

Silk was also given as payment to soldiers, who then traded the silk with nomads, who then traded the silk with others. You can easily see how silk became one of the most prominent goods traded along the famous trade route from the Silk Road's earliest point in known history.

As outside cultures saw the beauty of shimmering silk, they became hooked. Silk skyrocketed in popularity among the elite and wealthy as one of the most popular luxury goods to ever exist on planet Earth.

Silk left a lasting impact on the global economy. It bridged cultures, bringing together regions that would have otherwise likely been at war with each other (not to say that silk was a magical item that prevented war, but it did make empires think twice before attacking since it would impact trade). It boosted economies and inspired trade all across Asia and Europe. Today, silk is still a luxury good, with China still producing around 80 percent of the world's silk.

Spices

Have you ever come face to face with the ferocious Cinnamologus?

It is very likely you have not because this fabled bird lived some 2,500 years ago. Arab traders told the ancient Greeks and Romans how they used chunks of meat to trick the Cinnamologus and lure it away from the nest. When the Cinnamologus grabbed the big pieces of meat and flew back to its nest, the weight of the bird landing with the meat caused the big nest to collapse, scattering sticks of cinnamon for the traders to collect.

The cassia spice has a similar origin story. The Greek historian Herodotus said that cassia was collected in a lake that was protected by "winged creatures like bats, which screeched alarmingly and were very pugnacious."[13]

The international trade of spices along the Silk Road was very closely guarded by tradesmen. They did not want to share their secret sources for the spices for fear of others edging in on their sources. Thus, the tall tales were born, and they were even believed by people who lived far

---

[13] Herodotus. *Histories*.

away from the Eastern spice-growing lands.

Fantastical origin stories spread across Europe during the Middle Ages as people tried to understand where their spices came from. One story that still exists today tells us that cloves were gathered by nets from the Nile River in Egypt. People in the West had no idea where these spices packed full of flavor originated from, and the tradesmen wanted to keep it that way to secure their business.

Today, we can purchase almost any sort of spice or seasoning at the grocery store, in a cultural market, or even online with ease. Years ago, before our world was interconnected with travel, people were limited to what plants grew in their own regions. As you can imagine, this led to very little culinary variety.

The value of spices and dried herbs was exceedingly high for traders. They had multiple uses; for instance, they could be used for flavoring or medicine. Best of all, they were very easy to transport. Spices took up little space, which was important when traveling by caravan or sailing on a small boat. The value to weight ratio of spices made them a lucrative trade item.

The word "spices" is derived from the Latin term *species*, which translates to "special wares." Spices were no ordinary trade item; they were a little different than ordinary trade items and often far more valuable.

While spices were traded along the traditional land routes of the Silk Road, the most efficient and well-known spice trading was done along the maritime Silk Road routes. These sea routes stretched from the west coast of Japan, circled around the islands of Indonesia, made stops in India and the Middle East, then crossed the Mediterranean Sea to arrive in Europe, where spices spread across the continent all the way into present-day Great Britain. Historians say the spice trade marked the beginning of globalization.

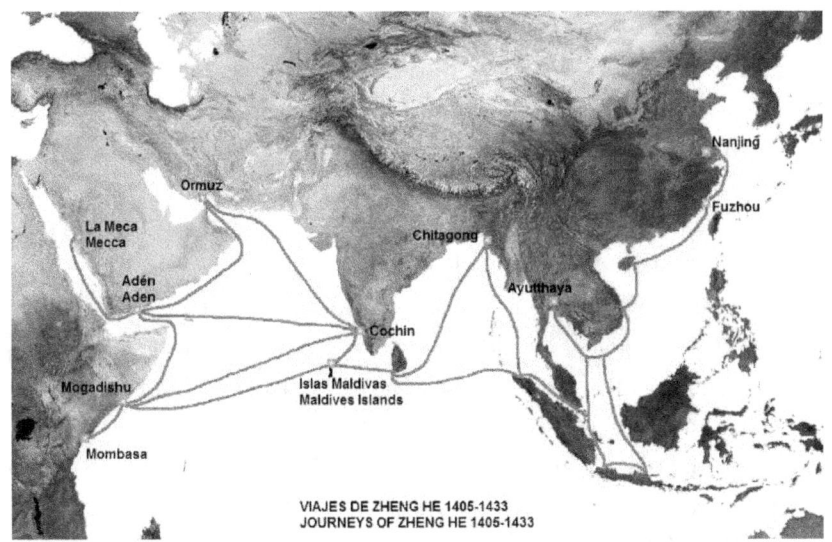

The maritime routes of the Silk Road. You can also see the routes taken by Zheng He, a Muslim admiral who explored Southeast Asia, the Middle East, and other regions in the 15th century. *Continentalis, CC BY-SA 3.0 <https://creativecommons.org/licenses/by-sa/3.0>, via Wikimedia Commons https://commons.wikimedia.org/wiki/File:Zheng_He.png*

What spices were traded along the Silk Road?

Most of the spices during the time of the Silk Road came from tropical plants that could only be grown in the heat and moisture of the Far East, not the cooler, dryer climates of Europe. In Europe, people could grow herbs like basil, mint, rosemary, and thyme, but the stronger spices came from the tropics, thousands of miles away, making them an exotic delicacy.

Among these spices were pepper, cloves, mace, and cumin. These spices were expensive, but affluent noblemen could afford them.

Pepper was transported in carefully guarded caravans because it was such a sought-after item. The Romans used pepper in their dishes in the 1st century CE. Peppercorns only grew along the coast of India and the Indonesian islands, so they could only reach Rome and Europe along the trade routes. Cloves, mace, and cumin were transported in the same manner as pepper. They were initially traded along maritime routes and then along the Silk Road in packs on the backs of camels or in wagons so they could be guarded from thieves.

The most valuable spices were worth more than their weight in gold. These spices were cinnamon, nutmeg, ginger, and saffron. These expensive spices were only available to the most elite people in society.

Kings used spices to show off the elaborate meals they could have, making these spices associated with riches and power.

The Arabs' hold as middlemen in the spice trade held out until 1498, when Portuguese explorer Vasco da Gama managed to sail around the southern tip of Africa to reach India for the first time in European history. This started a battle with the Arabs, who were not very happy to relinquish their grip on the spice trade.

Do you know what other famous explorers set sail in an attempt to reach India for spices?

Christopher Columbus was searching for pepper and a route to break into the spice trade when he took a wrong turn.

Without the elusive and luxurious spices from the Far East, global trade and exploration might have never been set in motion, altering history as we know it.

Spices on the Silk Road represented more than just excitement for one's taste buds. The spice trade shaped culinary traditions all along the trade route. Spices also serve as a marker for the transport of knowledge and culture along the Silk Road. Where the spices went, religious and cultural ideas followed, along with massive amounts of wealth.

Today, we can trace spices along the Silk Road based on shared gastronomic heritage. Not only do we find common dishes being made with similar ingredients all up and down the Silk Road, but we can also see common ideas as well. For example, the idea of hot and cold foods from Iran is the same in Chinese culture and is similar to the concept of ayurveda from India. This is a direct result of cultures blending together along the trade route!

Precious Metals and Gems

Speaking of massive amounts of wealth, spices were not the only money-making goods traded along the Silk Road. Accompanying the exotic spices from the Far East were eye-popping gemstones and precious metals that wowed the elite members of society in the West.

Deep in the Hindu Kush Mountains, even still in the present day, lies a mine in such a remote area that it only opens up for a few summer months out of the year. This mine is in Sar-e-Sang, a valley located in present-day Badakhshan, Afghanistan.

The gorgeous gemstone mined in Sar-e-Sang is called lapis lazuli. Greek philosopher Theophrastus, who lived from around 372 to 287

BCE, called lapis lazuli a sapphire spotted with gold.

Removing the deposits of lapis lazuli from deep within the Hindu Kush Mountains was a formidable task for miners. The mine's limestone rocks were so hard that ancient miners had to use fire to crack them in order to remove the gems. Lapis lazuli was mined in large blocks. These blocks were carried out of the mines on the backs of men, then transported by donkey to camps and then to a nearby village. The large blocks were eventually carved for trade.

Today, lapis lazuli is still removed from the mines in the exact same manner, on the backs of men and transported through the rough mountain terrain and high passes on donkeys to the nearest village.

Roman or Greek ring stone made of lapis lazuli.
Metropolitan Museum of Art, CC0, via Wikimedia Commons;
https://commons.wikimedia.org/wiki/File:Lapis_lazuli_ring_stone_MET_DP261442_(cropped).jpg

Lapis lazuli was considered a treasure in the ancient world. It has been found in archaeological sites in many places, including ancient Ur, Neolithic Mesopotamia, Greece, the Roman Empire, Egypt, and China. Lapis lazuli has been found in the tombs of only the wealthiest members of these societies. It was revered for its blue color, and it was used in rituals for many societies, including the Hebrews, Babylonians, and Assyrians.

Perhaps better known to the average person than lapis lazuli is the bright green gemstone called jade. Jade played a major role in diplomatic trade during the Tang dynasty and contributed to the factors that allowed the Silk Road to flourish and grow.

In China, jade was renowned for toolmaking and as a beautiful ritualistic gemstone. For the Chinese, jade represented the five qualities that every man should have: kindness, morality, wisdom, bravery, and purity. Jade was synonymous with the ideals of purity and indestructibility.

The indestructible aspect of jade made it the perfect material for tools in times before smelting and forging were possible. You may have heard of the Bronze Age, which occurred some five thousand years ago. Scholars say there was a lesser-known Jade Age that occurred alongside the Bronze Age in China and as far west as the Mediterranean due to the prevalence of jade toolmaking.

The Chinese exhausted their jade mines; you may be able to guess what happened next.

The route for trade was wide open.

The Chinese located another source of jade in Khotan in the far western part of China, along the Silk Road. Khotan became an important trade hub and a multicultural city. The city was known for being the first area outside of central China to farm mulberry trees, the food for the silkworms used to make silk threads. The people in Khotan also became famous for their carpets, which were as valuable as precious metals.

The trade for jade tools died down when China became a center of advanced bronze technology during the Bronze Age. However, jade remained a nearly sacred gem to Chinese culture throughout its history, and it still continues to play a significant role today.

In the West, we think of gold as the ultimate precious metal. In China and along the Silk Road, gold was valuable, though not as much as jade was, especially in China. Other items held as much, if not more, value than gold, such as silk or gemstones.

Gold and silver were both used as currencies for buying and selling goods on the Silk Road. Because the Silk Road was so long and went between many countries and cultures, it became necessary to exchange currencies between regions. One easy way to do this was by the weight of the gold or silver in a coin.

It did not matter where the coin came from. The value was simply determined by the weight, creating simple currency exchanges that spanned all regions of the Silk Road.

Gold and silver coins are long lasting and do not decay like other items traded along the Silk Road. This has left archaeologists with an amazing trail of evidence when it comes to trade. Gold and silver coins from multiple countries have been found all along the trade route, showing just how far people and their goods (and their coins!) were able to travel.

Coins from the Persian Empire and the Byzantine Empire have been found as far east as China, along with the bodies of foreign traders and foreign officials.

The Chinese were somewhat of an exception to the gold and silver currencies, as they preferred to use jade and silk in trade. Some evidence shows they might have worn gold coins as pendants.

Gold was worn in other Silk Road cultures as well. Gold was woven into silk, embroidered on garments, and, of course, made into jewelry. Gold was used as a symbol of wealth and status, similar to gemstones.

Gold on the Silk Road was mined along the Mediterranean, mainly in North Africa in the Sahara region. From there, the gold was traded for other goods like spices, clothing, silk, and gemstones. The gold then traveled back toward the Far East along the Silk Road, proving just how intricate the web of trade was.

Lapis lazuli was mined in blustery, cold, high-altitude mountains and sent down the Silk Road. In stark contrast, pearls were gathered from the warm Persian Gulf and joined the precious lapis lazuli on the trade route as a luxury item for the rich. Exceptionally high-quality pearls have been mentioned as far back as ancient Mesopotamia. They have also been found as far as India, central Asia, China, and Europe.

Overall, the cultural significance of both gemstones and precious metals that were mined and traded along the Silk Road was immeasurable. Alongside silk, gemstones and precious metals powered the diplomatic advances in regions of the Silk Road, paving the way for further trade and expansion.

Other Valuable Goods

Thus far, we have mentioned quite a few important trade goods on the Silk Road, such as silk, spices, gems, and precious metals. The Silk Road was like a one-stop shop, a large trade hub for everything you could possibly imagine (at least everything that could travel in a caravan or on a boat between remote regions).

Today, when we say the word porcelain, what comes to mind? For some of us, it will be the porcelain throne or the toilet. For others, we will think of fine china on a fancy table. During the time of the Silk Road, people associated porcelain with the country of China because the Chinese were prolific producers of these hard, translucent ceramics.

The porcelain trade began during the Tang dynasty during the initial expansion of the Silk Road. It started out as fine tableware and decorative items but soon expanded to gorgeous decorations and unique artwork produced by massive kilns during the Ming dynasty.

The love for porcelain spread along the Silk Road, and Chinese culture and artwork spread along with it. Chinese porcelain pottery had intricate designs that blended with the artwork of other cultures since the pottery was traded and shared from region to region.

For a number of years, the Chinese closely guarded their porcelain-making methods, similar to the way they kept the secret about silk's true origins. Eventually, other cultures learned how to make their own porcelain. The Persians had their own style of ceramics that was heavily influenced by Chinese porcelain.

What do you think people were drinking out of their fine porcelain cups? If you immediately thought of tea, you would be correct! Tea leaves were yet another famous good traded along the Silk Road.

Once again, our journey begins deep within China, this time around 2737 BCE. At some point during this legendary year, Emperor Shennong was minding his own business while boiling some water underneath a tree.

As fate would have it, a few leaves from a *Camellia sinensis* plant nearby were knocked off by a gust of wind and landed right into his pot of boiling water.

The result was quite a surprise. It had a pleasant taste, and as legend goes, it also had medicinal properties. This was the first pot of tea ever made.

From this point on, tea was cultivated from the leaves of the *Camellia sinensis* plant. From the 16th to the 3rd century BCE, the Chinese perfected the cultivation of tea leaves, and they began transporting dried leaves around the region. During the Tang dynasty, tea exploded in popularity, and tea houses opened for business.

At this point, tea leaves began to travel down the Silk Road, spreading into other nearby cultures. Eventually, tea became an internationally known beverage. The sweet tea people drink today in the southern United States would never have been possible if tea had not taken a journey down the Silk Road!

There was one more very important item that traveled down the Silk Road that completely changed history as we know it. Yes, furs, livestock, textiles, foods, and even slaves were traded on the Silk Road, but what about paper?

The Chinese yet again burst onto the scene with a world-shattering discovery: papermaking.

The earliest Chinese paper was made with materials like mulberry bark, bamboo, and hemp, which were pounded into a pulp, moistened with water, and spread thin to dry.

At first, paper was a luxury reserved only for important official documents, writings, and special artwork. Over time, paper mills were established across China, making paper more common and accessible.

Initially, paper on the Silk Road was a novel concept. It soon caught on, as scholars began writing down their knowledge and sharing it from city to city along the Silk Road.

Religious texts were also shared through paper. In 751 CE, Arabs captured Chinese prisoners of war during the Battle of Talas. It is believed this was the first time papermaking knowledge reached the Muslims. The Islamic world was particularly fond of paper, taking the Chinese method and adding cotton and linen fibers to create something softer and more pliable.

Paper changed the world in obvious ways. Knowledge could now be written down in books and shared across wide distances. Paper was perfectly suited for travel on a trade route. It was not until the 12th century that the Muslims in Spain created their own paper mills, allowing the knowledge of papermaking to spread across Europe.

Paper, porcelain, and tea leaves traveled from Asia along the Silk Road to Europe, but what was coming back to Asia in return? The Chinese valued wool and woven textiles from Europe for their good quality. Horses were traded between the two regions as well. Herbs, which were used for their medicinal properties, were also imported to China from Europe along the Silk Road. Wine from Rome was sent to the East. Precious metals like gold and silver were also traded, along with amber that was sourced from Europe.

Chapter 5: The Travelers of the Silk Road

Perhaps the most famous European traveler along the Silk Road is Marco Polo. His fame lay in doing exactly what most travelers on the Silk Road did not do. That is, he allegedly traveled the entire route from start to finish.

Instead, the average traveler would only go a short distance from place to place, from city to city, or from trading point to trading point. Many of these people were just traders who moved goods from one place to the next and took their cut out of the price.

In some situations, people created entire caravans to travel as a group. This was often for protection against attack and theft. Caravans were most commonly used to cross the desert regions of the Silk Road for strength in numbers.

Let us take a look at what might have gone into creating an ancient Silk Road caravan.

First, we have to consider that not all caravans were exactly the same. The contents of the caravan varied widely depending on the destination, the goods they were carrying, and a number of other factors.

Let us say we were organizing a caravan through the desert. We would take Bactrian camels as our main source of transportation.

Bactrian camels have two humps and two coats of hair. The first coat of hair is the outer layer that faces the elements. The second coat of hair is the inner layer that protects the skin. This layer of hair should never get wet. The space between the two layers creates a pocket of air that holds warmth or protects the body from heat, making these camels ideal for travel in extreme climates like the desert, where it could be hot during the day and very cold at night.

These impressive beasts also have two sets of eyelids and eyelashes to protect them against sandstorms and desert dust. The second set of eyelids functions as a sort of windshield wiper, smoothing away debris during a sandstorm. The camel's nostrils can shrink down to narrow slits during sandstorms to protect the lungs from choking on sand.

The Bactrian camel has other special features that allow it to travel long distances across inhospitable deserts. These hardy camels can go up to one week without any water and up to a month without food!

The secret lies within their two humps. The humps store up to one hundred pounds of fat each! When the humps are full to the brim with fat, they can rise eighteen inches off of the camel's body. As the fat stores are used up, the humps shrink down lower and lower.

In our caravan through the desert, we would tie at least two camels or maybe more, possibly up to six of them, together, nose to tail.

The camels will be carefully loaded with the goods we want to trade or sell. Camels are grumpy creatures and will complain if they are uncomfortable, so we would need to load them just right. To load the goods, we would use some cargo racks or baskets that we tie on with blankets to the camel's backs.

Riding on the first camel is our caravan leader. This person is a man who has several important qualities. First, he is a skilled guide who knows his way through the sand dunes. He knows the location of hidden wells and outposts along the way. He does not use a map or a compass. Instead, he travels by following familiar routes and landmarks and using the North Star as a guide. He knows our camels prefer to go across the tops of the dunes rather than waste energy going up and down them.

Second, he is a skilled talker. He is great at negotiating and trading.

As for those of us in the caravan, we might walk sometimes. Later, we will climb on the camels' shoulders to ride. Some of us will bring horses. The wind is so strong in the desert that we will not talk much. We will have a cloth over our noses and mouths to keep blowing sand out.

We will travel through the hot day until after dark when it begins to get cold. Then, we will stop to unload the camels so they can rest. To keep the camels from wandering off, we will hobble their feet with rope. Once the camels are unloaded, someone will build a fire, and we will cook whatever we have brought along on the journey to eat—probably some stew or grains boiled over the flames or maybe some onions, peppers, or goat meat we got at the last oasis stop.

In the morning, we will eat the leftovers for breakfast before loading up the camels again and continuing on our journey. We brought some dates to eat for lunch while riding.

Riding in a caravan was not as easy as it sounds here. We have to keep the camels moving at the exact same pace, or they will tangle their ropes and break them, creating a disaster. The last thing we would want is a runaway camel carrying precious cargo in the middle of the sand dunes.

We also have to constantly be on the lookout for bandits who are looking to steal our goods, our coins, or even our camels.

We brought grass with us, which we use to sleep on at night and feed to the camels. We find camel ticks crawling on us and biting us, which is very unpleasant.

When we reach an oasis in the desert, the camels find palm fronds or scrubby trees to munch on. They can drink twenty-five to thirty gallons of water in one sitting!

When we reach a caravanserai, we feel excitement and relief. We see a set of buildings with a courtyard full of animals tied out on wooden stakes and a covered market area.

This is a stopping place on the Silk Road. There is an inn to sleep in, a stable for our animals, and plenty of food and water. We are going to spend about a week resting here before tackling the rest of our long journey. We need the camels and horses to fatten up a little bit.

This place also has a lot of people to trade with. There are brothels here, people from multiple different cultures, and impressive market stalls to shop in. We can sleep at the inn, and we have to pay a fee for our animals to stay in the stable and eat. The owners collect the manure from our animals to sell as fuel or compost, which allows the courtyard to stay clean.

Eventually, we will move on and travel through the desert again for a few days until we reach the next stop along our route.

Who Traveled the Silk Road?

A camel caravan.
https://commons.wikimedia.org/wiki/File:Richard_Zommer_-_Camel_Caravan_with_Travelling_Family.jpg

Those who made the perilous journeys along the Silk Road came from a wide variety of backgrounds. Some were simply tradesmen who lived in the area and regularly traveled from one trade point to the next. These were the middlemen who were responsible for changing goods from hand to hand along the route.

Scholars traveled along the trade routes for a variety of reasons. If a scholar was in search of a certain religious text, he would have to journey along the Silk Road in order to find it.

Some people took pilgrimages to sacred religious sites. This included Hindus, Buddhists, Christians, and Muslims, among others.

Scholars who studied different cultures and religions would travel the Silk Road in search of new people and places to observe and document. These scholars contributed mightily to the exchange of cross-cultural ideas.

Many caravanserais were meeting places for scholars to spend time sharing their ideas in person so they could learn from each other. They wrote together, shared poetry and stories, held debates, and pooled together results from studies they had conducted. Scholars also traveled the Silk Road to study botany, astronomy, and geographical features, which they also shared with each other at meeting points along the route.

Artists would draw what they saw along the route and observe the different cultures they came into contact with along the way. Philosophers gained new insights and shared them with others. Translators were able to get their hands on different manuscripts and rewrite them in other languages so that ideas could be shared with even more cultures.

The Silk Road played a vital role in the spread of knowledge and ideas, creating a melting pot of knowledge and culture for people to partake in.

While most people know of Marco Polo, few have heard about Abu Abdullah Muhammad Ibn Battuta. Commonly known as Ibn Battuta, he was a young man born in Tangier, Morocco, on February 24th, 1304 CE.

A sketch of what Ibn Battuta might have looked like.
https://commons.wikimedia.org/wiki/File:Ibn_Battuta,_Sayr_mulhimah_min_al-Sharq_wa-al-Gharb.png

Ibn Battuta was a scholar who set out to travel the Silk Road in search of knowledge. He was gone on his journey for more than thirty years. During his travels, which took place from 1325 to 1354, Islam was expanding rapidly outside of modern-day Saudia Arabia, with religious ideas traveling along the Silk Road and into outlying territories.

Ibn Battuta first traveled to Mecca as a religious pilgrimage for his Muslim faith. He journeyed to Algiers and Tunis in North Africa. He also went to Egypt, where he visited twenty-two different cities, including Cairo and Alexandria. He then traveled through Palestine and Syria in the Middle East before eventually reaching Mecca in the Arabian Peninsula.

During his trip, he documented everything and made observations about his experiences. He was known as the Muslim traveling judge and a legal scholar.

His travels were not purely religious. Ibn Battuta wanted to find knowledge and visit libraries. He dreamed of going to the libraries of Cairo, Alexandria, and Damascus.

In Tunis (or possibly Mecca), he became a paid judge called a qadi, who traveled with caravans to settle their disputes. Ibn Battuta traveled to many different regions, living his life to the fullest. He married at least ten times during his travels and fathered multiple children while traveling along the Silk Road.

He journeyed through the Hindu Kush Mountains to reach India, where he asked the king of India for an official career. He became a judge of Delhi, but he grew bored after eight years. Ibn Battuta got the king of India to make him an ambassador to China, allowing him to continue his travels along the Silk Road.

Once Ibn Battuta returned home some thirty years later, he wrote a book detailing his adventures. It was titled *The Travels of Ibn Battuta: In the Near East, Asia and Africa.*

Who else traveled along the Silk Road?

Well, soldiers frequented the Silk Road for a number of reasons. First and foremost, soldiers would be sent to guard important caravans against bandits or rival tribes.

Soldiers were used as police of sorts to guard the caravanserais or settlements against chaos since tired and hungry people from a wide range of backgrounds all came together in one place.

The soldiers were also given the task of collecting taxes and checking for smugglers in some regions. Of course, one might also find soldiers traveling the Silk Road for average military purposes. They went between regions during battles and to prepare for incoming threats. Military outposts were established at various points along the Silk Road by local governments so they could have prepared military bases when they were needed.

There was another group of people that often traveled the Silk Road: slaves.

Arguably, slaves could be called one of the world's oldest currencies. The Silk Road was also referred to as the Slave Road for good reason.

Slaves during the time of the Silk Road were used for many purposes. They were often used as laborers for agriculture and farming or for domestic labor in rich households. When big projects were under way, like the construction of a new canal or bridge, slaves were brought in to help complete the project. Slaves were sometimes prisoners of war. Women and children could be slaves; they were often captured when a settlement was seized. Slaves also filled the brothels in caravanserais and city settlements.

From the 7th to the 9th century CE, it is estimated that 80 percent of caravans had slaves. It has also been recently estimated that 39 percent of travelers on the Silk Road in central Asia were traveling as slaves.[14] Most of these slaves were children from impoverished families.

Historians and archaeologists are still learning more about human trafficking on the Silk Road in ancient times. Recently, slaveholder contracts have been found in tombs in the Turfan region. The Turfan region was an ancient oasis city on the Silk Road in the present-day Xinjiang region of China. These contracts give historians clues about the ages of slaves on the Silk Road, as well as whether they were male or female.

The greatest slave trade in history occurred on the Silk Road when the Mongols transported Caucasians, Tartars, and Slavs to Crimea on the Black Sea to be sold as slaves.

Human trafficking is a lesser talked about but very important "good" traded on the Silk Road. Enslaved people were just as valued as silk, paper, and gemstones. In fact, regional governments that profited from import taxes on basic goods like silk and spices also taxed slaves in the same manner.

---

[14] "Slave Trade on the Silk Road." https://shanghai.nyu.edu/news/exploring-silk-road-slave-trade-turfan.

Human trafficking was present on the Silk Road for the entirety of its history. Even in the Middle Ages, a significant number of Europeans were trafficked along the Silk Road in exchange for silver. The slave trade was a booming business all across the spine of Asia and into Africa and Europe for thousands of years, operating as a hidden thread that boosted the wealth of empires on the Silk Road.

In the end, when we look back at our timeline of history and view the bigger picture, the travelers of the Silk Road were more than just random people who participated in trade. They were important to the culture and history of many regions, some traveling willingly and others traveling by force. However, each person participated in shaping the religions and cultures of many places in central Asia for centuries.

Chapter 6: The Silk Road: Art and Architecture

The Silk Road is home to thousands of years of human history. Some of the many clues left behind for historians and archaeologists are sealed in tombs or written down in surviving manuscripts. Other valuable insights have been left behind for us to explore in the form of buildings and artwork.

The architecture left along the Silk Road gives us information about the values of the people who lived in the area and tells the story of how they lived their daily lives.

Some aspects of architecture on the Silk Road are the same in every place, regardless of the culture and the location. This is because the architecture was designed to meet a specific need of the travelers. The finer details of aesthetics, such as the materials used and the style, were left up to the local culture.

Caravanserais

Caravanserais, the places created along the Silk Road for travelers to rest their animals and sleep, are all arranged in the exact same manner no matter where they are located on the trade route. Each location consisted of a circle of buildings with a courtyard in the center for animals.

A caravanserai in Iran.
Bernard Gagnon, CC BY-SA 4.0 <https://creativecommons.org/licenses/by-sa/4.0>, via Wikimedia Commons; https://commons.wikimedia.org/wiki/File:Izadkhvast_Caravanserai_01.jpg

We know that many of the cities that developed along the Silk Road were originally oases and trade hubs. They grew over time into large, prosperous cities due to the economic benefits of trade.

Palmyra, a city that blossomed in the middle of the desolate Tadmorean Desert, is one such city. In the present day, the ruins of Palmyra's Silk Road architecture can be found in Syria. Unfortunately, recent wars have brought unknown amounts of destruction to many of these historic ruins.

Palmyra is a true caravan city, growing out of a crisscross of caravan trails in no-man's land. The initial infrastructure of this desert oasis was developed to meet the needs of people who were passing through the area on the Silk Road. Palmyra had a public meeting place in the city center known as the agora, which was probably built during the 1st century. The style of the agora matches the architecture of other Greco-Roman cities.[15]

The buildings of Palmyra were constructed from beautiful pale gold limestone gathered from the local landscape. The market, built for trade as travelers passed through, had a magnificent colonnade. The colonnade had around 375 columns that were 31 feet (9.5 meters) in height.

---

[15] https://en.unesco.org/silkroad/content/palmyra

The artwork found in Palmyra gives further evidence of Greek and Roman influence over this Middle Eastern city. Sculptures match the Greek style of the time period. Greek and Parthian clothing styles have been found in the ruins of Palmyra.

The Greek clothing for men included a long linen tunic with a cloth that went down to the elbows and a large cloak made of linen or wool. Archaeologists also discovered remnants of Chinese silk.

The Parthian clothing was different. It included a long-sleeved tunic worn with pants that were tight around the ankles. Parthian clothing was also worn with a cloak over the top and included a belt and boots. The cloth had ornate patterns, setting it apart from the Greek style.

Palmyra was most certainly a multicultural city with its gorgeous architecture and various clothing styles. The Greek influence was heavy, as caravans often filtered into Palmyra from the west. Inscriptions inside the architecture and in the graveyard were in several languages, such as Greek and Aramaic. In later years, they were also in Latin.

Mosques

Another fabulous example of architecture and art spreading from region to region via the Silk Road is the Hagia Sophia in Istanbul, Turkey, with its massive 180-foot dome. First built in 532 by Emperor Justinian, it was the largest Christian church in the world for quite some time.

A photo of Hagia Sophia from 2013.
Arild Vågen, CC BY-SA 3.0 <https://creativecommons.org/licenses/by-sa/3.0>, via Wikimedia Commons; https://commons.wikimedia.org/wiki/File:Hagia_Sophia_Mars_2013.jpg

After the Ottomans conquered the area and converted the Hagia Sophia into a mosque in 1453, they added four minarets to the mosque. Visitors from all over came to visit the Hagia Sophia and saw its splendor before traveling to other regions.[16]

The Sultanahmet Mosque was built nearby in the same style, with a dome and four minarets. Silk Road trade is evident in this mosque as well because of the twenty thousand blue-painted İznik tiles in the interior, which first gained popularity when people traveled the Silk Road years before.

What is unique about these handmade blue tiles?

The Mongols, led by one Genghis Khan, reached neighboring Iran in 1220. With them came Chinese art and architecture, including knowledge of ceramic making.

The people of Constantinople had gained a taste for fine Chinese ceramics. Soon, they began trading ceramics with China. During the Ming dynasty, the famous blue and white Ming porcelains heavily influenced the design of the blue İznik tiles inside the Sultanahmet Mosque.

This mosque was built in the same style as the previous mosques, with a dome and minarets. It even included the color blue, which represented water. The blue exterior became a key feature of Persian domes.

Persian Islamic design influenced mosques all along the Silk Road, but the architecture of the mosques was not the only feature that spread from city to city. Impressive gardens were also popular and could be found accompanying beautiful architecture up and down the Silk Road.

In present-day southeast Uzbekistan, weary Silk Road travelers found the city of Samarkand. The Bibi-Khanym Mosque in Samarkand has a massive dome that was built using ninety-five elephants from India. It was finished in 1404. This mosque had eight minarets and a three-walled turquoise blue dome with a tiled interior.

We can follow the unbroken link of the Silk Road by looking at the architecture from place to place. For instance, the Bibi-Khanym Mosque was a direct influence on the design of perhaps the most famous building

---

[16] https://www.saga.co.uk/magazine/travel/destinations/asia/central-asia/silk-road-islamic-architecture

in India: the Taj Mahal in Agra.

Hints of Istanbul and Samarkand can be clearly seen in India when viewing the Taj Mahal, but let us not forget about the gardens! The Taj Mahal also has a large garden divided into four segments, just like the gardens of Persia. Each garden features shade and running water. These gardens were supposed to remind people of paradise.

The Taj Mahal has a large water feature with a carefully designed reflection that creates symmetry. The gardens of the Taj Mahal resemble the gardens of Samarkand, with their division into quarters and a pavilion in the center.

The Silk Road's influence spanned thousands of miles, even reaching into far eastern China, where mosques began to appear. However, the Chinese mosques were not domed. They had more of a Buddhist style of architecture.

The Great Mosque of Xi'an was built using local wood and has a single three-story minaret in an octagonal shape. At first glance, a traveler may not see the link to the domed mosques of the Middle East. But take a closer look, and you will find that the unbroken chain of influence along the Silk Road still stands strong. The prayer hall has a roof made with glazed turquoise tile, giving a nod to the blue tiles of the domed mosques in Samarkand and beyond.

Stupas

Take a leap backward on our timeline of history, a time before Islam and mosques came through the Silk Road. Buddhist stupas were prevalent on the trade route, first emerging from India and spreading east into China. Each stupa and its artwork left behind clues to the places people traveled based on its architectural influence and inscriptions.

You may be wondering what a stupa is, especially if you live in the Western Hemisphere. Stupa is the Sanskrit word for *heap*. The first stupas were simply burial mounds containing a bit of the Buddha's ashes.

Over time, stupa architecture expanded to be burial mounds with rocks. India's King Ashoka (r. 269-232 BCE) built more than eighty-four thousand stupas all over India, Nepal, Pakistan, Bangladesh, and Afghanistan.

The Great Stupa (Mahastupa) was built at the birthplace of King Ashoka's wife, Devi. It was located along a major Silk Road trade route in Madya Pradesh, India.

The Great Stupa at Sanchi.
Biswarup Ganguly, CC BY 3.0 <https://creativecommons.org/licenses/by/3.0>, via Wikimedia Commons; https://commons.wikimedia.org/wiki/File:East_Gateway_-_Stupa_1_-_Sanchi_Hill_2013-02-21_4398.JPG

The stupa has a domed roof, which predates the spread of Islam and the domed mosques. Unlike the mosques, the stupa is not meant to be entered. It is a solid mound that a person walks around.

The southern route of the Silk Road along the Tarim Basin in northwestern China had stupas with northwestern Indian architectural features. That is quite a long distance for knowledge and ideas to travel!

Buddhist statues give us more clues as to the influence of art on the Silk Road. The Bamiyan Valley is an isolated region high in the Hindu Kush Mountains of Afghanistan. This area became a major link along the Silk Road between India and China.

There, archaeologists discovered ancient Buddhist statues with blatant evidence of influence from the trade route. The Kushans who lived in this area became middlemen in the trade between China, India, and

Rome. They seamlessly blended their tribal culture with their trade partners, leaving behind an unforgettable cultural legacy.

The central Asian traditions fused with Hellenistic art from the Greek Mediterranean region, and this blended into Buddhist religious practices coming out of India.

Evidence of this is clearly shown in the art and statues left behind. The Buddha statues of Bamiyan display Roman clothing. A stupa called Tope Darra (or Topdara), located in the mountains north of Kabul, contains statues with Hellenistic features.

In 2001, the Taliban destroyed two large Buddha figures from the 5th century outside of Bamiyan. These two statues stood together in cliffside niches, with artificially created caves surrounding them in the cliffs. Inside the caves were artistic influences from India and Iran, along with Hellenistic art and Greek influences.

The chain of influence from the Silk Road spread smoothly from tribe to tribe and from region to region as items were traded between people groups over the trade route, leaving behind artwork displaying a fascinating fusion of cultures.

In 970 CE, Bamiyan was conquered by the Muslims, and Islam arrived in the region. The blend of religious and cultural influences continued for hundreds of years as domed stupas gave way to domed mosques.

Ancient pagoda in Sidoktaya.
https://commons.wikimedia.org/wiki/File:Ancient_Pagoda_in_Sidoktaya.JPG

In addition to stupas, the Buddhists also created Chinese pagodas. These evolved out of stupas. Pagodas were larger buildings that could be entered, unlike the stupas, which were mounds containing relics that could only be circled by visitors. Both pagodas and stupas were memorials to pay respect to the famous and important Buddhists who had died, including the Buddha himself.

In Xi'an, China, the famous Big Wild Goose Pagoda still stands. It was first built in 652 CE during the Tang dynasty and then rebuilt in 704. It climbs seven stories high.

Do you know what the main function of this pagoda was and still is today? The pagoda holds statues of Gautama Buddha, which were brought back to China by a man named Xuanzang in the 7th century. He was a scholar, traveler, and translator. These statues of Buddha are renowned in China, and they traveled along the Silk Road from India.

Statue of Xuanzang in front of Big Wild Goose Pagoda.

John Hill, CC BY-SA 4.0 <https://creativecommons.org/licenses/by-sa/4.0>, via Wikimedia Commons; https://commons.wikimedia.org/wiki/File:Statue_of_Xuanzang_in_front_of_Giant_Wild_Goose_Pagoda,_Xi%27an,_2011.jpg

Today, Big Wild Goose Pagoda is a World Heritage Site. It was added in 2014 as part of the "Silk Roads: The Routes Network of Chang'an-Tianshan Corridor," which aims to preserve the heritage of the Silk Road in the Chang'an-Tianshan region of the route. There are thirty-three sites along the route, which spans more than 3,106 miles (5,000 kilometers) through China, Kazakhstan, and Kyrgyzstan.

Other regions along the Silk Road are also identified as World Heritage Sites, with each region made up of countries that submit applications for sites to UNESCO for approval.

Mogao Caves

The Mogao Caves.
Zhangzhugang, CC BY-SA 4.0 <https://creativecommons.org/licenses/by-sa/4.0>, via Wikimedia Commons; https://commons.wikimedia.org/wiki/File:Dunhuang_Mogao_Ku_2013.12.31_12-30-18.jpg

Even Buddhist cave art has elements of other regions incorporated into it. The Mogao Caves, also known as the Thousand Buddha Grottoes or Caves of the Thousand Buddhas, are located in what was an oasis of the Silk Road in present-day Gansu Province, China, outside of the city of Dunhuang. This crossroads was a place where many cultures mixed together, as evidenced by the artwork inside of the caves.

It is estimated that the artwork inside of the caves spans more than one thousand years of history. These caves were dug out, so they are fully manmade, not natural caves. The first cave was dug out in 366 CE, with construction of the caves continuing all the way until the 14th century! Today, there remain more than five hundred connected temples inside of the cave system.

These caves were used for worship and meditation by Buddhists who lived and traveled in the region. The most amazing aspect of the Mogao Caves is the artwork contained within them. These caves have more than 400,000 square feet of frescos and sculptures. In fact, there is so much art in the caves that it covers ten major genres, including architecture, stucco sculpture, wall paintings, silk paintings, calligraphy, woodblock printing, embroidery, literature, music, and dance.

A cave mural of Zhang Qian traveling along the Silk Road.
https://commons.wikimedia.org/wiki/File:Zhang_Qian.jpg

The cave murals display rich, intricate artwork and fill cave chambers from floor to ceiling. The influence of Buddhist artwork can be clearly seen in the cave paintings. The earliest paintings display characteristics from India and central Asia in the painting style and clothing worn in the portraits. However, a distinct local painting style began to emerge, blending together cultures.

The Mogao Caves also contain unique architecture. You may not think of a cave system as having architectural features, but these caves certainly do. The earliest caves are similar to rock-cut caves found in India, like the Ajanta Caves. This style features a square central column with cut-outs meant to hold sculptures. This style represents the stupa architecture since visitors were supposed to walk in a circle around the memorial statues.

Another type of architectural design found in the cave system is hall caves. These caves had pyramid-shaped ceilings meant to resemble a tent. Some of them had flat carved ceilings resembling that of a building.

The third architectural type represented in the caves is the vihara cave plan, which was the monastery style from India. These caves were used for meditation. Each one contains side chambers that are only large enough for one person to sit inside to meditate.

The city of Dunhuang itself is a strategic point on the intricate web of trade routes. It lay at a crossroads between two major trade routes of the Silk Road. It sits on an oasis in the Taklamakan Desert, poised against Crescent Lake and Mingsha Shan on the western edge of the Gobi Desert. In Chinese, Mingsha Shan means "Singing Sand Mountain." This site was named after the singing noise made by the wind hitting the sand dunes in the desert.

Imagine traveling through the desert and arriving at this oasis city. As your exhausted caravan pulls closer to the town, you are anxious to see China for the first time (Dunhuang was the first Chinese city travelers encountered on the Silk Road when coming from India in the west). All you can hear is the sound of the dunes singing in the whipping desert wind.

The first part of the city you would reach is the Jade Gate, a garrison erected to protect this important trade city from invaders. Inside the gates, you find a melting pot of humanity. Tradesmen, Buddhist scholars, and craftsmen all meet here.

Dunhuang produced a number of goods to sell or trade on the Silk Road. It was a big producer of silk and not just one type of silk either. The people there produced several different varieties. The city also had cotton and wool from the surrounding regions. The people used these textiles and created beautiful embroidery. They also produced and sold furs, tea leaves, various medicines, jade objects, camels, sheep, dried fruits, dyes, and tools.

The city was full of different languages, thanks to the tradesmen coming in from the Silk Road. Scrolls found in the library cave of the Mogao Caves give us clues about the people who passed through the city. Chinese and Tibetan were regularly spoken in the city. Sanskrit, Khotanese, Uighur, and Sogdian were also used.

The scrolls also hint that Dunhuang was a city where multiple religions lived side by side. The main religion was Buddhism, but Judaism, Zoroastrianism, Manichaeism, Christianity, and Daoism were also part of the city's vibrant culture.

Outside of China, there are quite a few other UNESCO World Heritage Sites on the Silk Road that people can visit today. Many of these sites have been damaged or destroyed due to weather, earthquakes, and wars. Work is being done by many countries around the world to preserve what is left of the unique cultural heritage left behind by the Silk Road.

Chapter 7: Religion and the Silk Road

Religion along the Silk Road was continually fluid, spreading in ripples and waves and blending with local tribal traditions. Different faiths often coexisted side by side in multicultural oasis cities, but more often than not, religions competed with each other until a winner took over and swept along the Silk Road, bringing with it the artistic and architectural influences we discussed in the previous chapter.

Zoroastrianism

This ancient religion was said to be the precursor to the three major Abrahamic religions: Judaism, Christianity, and Islam. Many consider it the father of monotheistic religion.

Zoroaster was one of the first documented people to reject the idea of multiple gods and instead placed faith in one singular god. His god was known as Ahura Mazda, or the Lord of Wisdom. He believed there was an evil force at work in the universe called Ahriman.

Zoroaster was born sometime between the 11th and 6th century BCE in the region of Mongolia and Azerbaijan, but it was not until well after his death in the 3rd century that Zoroastrianism became the official religion of the region when Iran was ruled by the Sasanian dynasty in the Persian Empire.

Zoroastrianism spread down the Silk Road. The religion also made it into the philosophies and teachings of Hellenistic Greece. Though the Greeks had secondhand information that was sometimes incorrect, it is remarkable that Zoroaster's influence was strong enough to appear in writings from classical Greek philosophers several centuries later.

Herodotus, who lived from 484 to 425 BCE, was known as the "Father of History." He wrote about Zoroaster in his book titled *Histories*. Herodotus noted that Zoroaster was a teacher of wisdom and wrote about him as a historical figure who impacted Persian religions.

The Hellenistic Greek geographer Strabo (64-24 CE) wrote about Zoroaster in his work *Geographica* (*Geography*), saying he was a religious leader and philosopher.

At one point in time, a fellow scholar accused Plato of plagiarizing the work of Zoroaster, though no proof has ever been found.

Pliny the Elder was a Roman author and naturalist who lived from 23 to 79 CE. He also wrote about Zoroaster in a similar context to Herodotus, noting that Zoroaster was influential in Persian religions and was a wise teacher. He also goes as far as to name Zoroaster as the inventor of magic, a wild claim that took hold and spread along the Silk Road. It is believed that Zoroaster inspired the Chaldean doctrines of astrology and magic.

A work attributed to Zoroaster about astronomy and predictions that contained five papyrus rolls was also in circulation at some point during the classical Greek and Roman periods.

Despite these claims and what amounts to ancient rumors that have lasted through the ages, all of the talk of magic and astronomy has very little to do with actual Zoroastrianism.

During the time of influential Zoroastrianism, there were many overlaps with other religions found in cultures along the Silk Road. For example, both Zoroastrianism and Hinduism use fire for their rituals.

Many other religions that evolved during the same time period overlapped with Zoroastrianism. The theory of duality—that is, a world with both good and evil—was a major feature of Zoroastrianism and the Abrahamic religions.

Zoroastrianism has persisted to the present day despite being marginalized by the spread of Judaism, Christianity, and Islam on the Silk Road. Today, there are isolated pockets of Zoroastrians in Iran, as well as descendants of Persian immigrants in India, where they are known as Parsis or Parsees. The number of adherents to Zoroastrianism totals around 100,000 to 200,000 people worldwide.

Christianity

During the 1st and 2nd centuries CE, small pockets of Christianity began to appear on the Silk Road. The religion did not travel in a steady wave; rather, it ebbed and flowed, working its way into local religions and slowly pushing out other beliefs.

The Apostle Thomas wrote about his travels to India. He might have also reached other parts of Asia. It is very likely Thomas was one of the Silk Road travelers. Christianity was spread by missionaries who purposefully traveled to spread the gospel far and wide.

Nestorian Christians were some of the first Christians to establish themselves along the Silk Road.[17] This branch of Christianity was slightly different from the mainstream Christianity most of us know today. They had several major theological differences, including the belief that Jesus had a divine nature and a human nature. Known as the Church of the East, they had their own hierarchy separate from the Byzantine and Roman Christian churches.

Archaeologists discovered significant proof that early Christianity was present in China during the Tang dynasty. The Nestorian Stele in Xi'an, China, is a stone monument standing thirty feet (nine meters) tall with an inscription describing the arrival of early Christianity in China. The inscription is written in two languages: Chinese and Syriac. Syriac was a form of Aramaic used in ancient China.

The stele also depicts crosses in intricately carved stone. It tells the story of how Christianity arrived in China. Surprisingly, it was not brought along the Silk Road. Christianity was brought to China by a Persian missionary named Alopen.

Are you surprised that Christianity arrived in China all the way from Persia?

Another surprising factoid is that the emperor of the Tang dynasty, Taizong, is thanked in the inscription for the support and patronage he pledged when the Christian community was established in China. The stele can still be viewed today in Xi'an, China; it is housed in the Xi'an Stele Forest Museum.

Perhaps one of the most pivotal roles in the spread of Christianity was played by Roman Emperor Constantine the Great. Under previous

---

[17] https://factsanddetails.com/china/cat2/sub90/entry-8324.html

Roman emperors, Christians had been persecuted. Constantine enacted the Edict of Milan in 313 CE, along with his co-ruler, Licinius. Constantine ruled the eastern half of Rome, and Licinius ruled the western half. Together, they agreed on religious tolerance for the empire as a whole.

This edict ended all persecution of Christians and granted religious tolerance to Christianity in the Roman Empire. Thus, the previously unwelcomed religion of Christianity pivoted from a persecuted sect of people to an acceptable religion within the Roman Empire, paving the way for Christianity to explode from west to east along the Silk Road.

Islam

Christianity was present in multiple communities along the Silk Road by the 1st century CE, although it would take a few hundred years for the religion to truly become popular with people. Several centuries later, Islam stormed the scene. The Prophet Muhammad began sharing his teachings in the Arabian Peninsula in the 7th century CE.

The Silk Road is almost entirely responsible for the spread of Islam throughout the world. Arabs were known for their sailing skills. If you remember when we discussed the spice trade in a previous chapter, you will know that the Arabs had a corner on that market. They came up with fantastical stories to trick their customers, hiding the true origin of the spices they sold.

When Islam took hold of the Arabian Peninsula in the 7th century CE, those Arab sailors were also affected. As they followed the maritime Silk Road trade routes into the Far East to buy spices, they stopped at ports along the way, where they shared information about the Prophet Muhammad.

The traders also brought their new religion to the Spice Islands along the coast of India, where they bought and traded rare spices to bring to the West. Inevitably, some of the merchants stayed in Indonesia to live with the local people, establishing Islam as a religion on the island.

Nearby Sumatra and the Philippines were influenced in the same manner. The king of Sumatra converted to Islam in the 12th century CE, and tombstones have been found with Islamic inscriptions by the 13th century.[18] Islam was the first monotheistic religion to take hold in the

---

[18] https://slate.com/news-and-politics/2005/01/how-islam-got-to-the-philippines.html

Philippines.[19]

Today, Islam is the second most widely practiced religion in the Philippines; Christianity is the most popular religion. Islam is mainly concentrated in the Bangsamoro region of the islands, where around 91 percent of the people are Sunni Muslims, though Muslims only make up around 6 percent of the total population of the Philippines.

Further commerce along the Silk Road also brought Brunei and Malaysia into the Islamic fold. Islam began to spread quickly through these eastern islands.

However, not every interaction with Islam on the Silk Road was peaceful. Over a few hundred years, Islam spread like wildfire from the Arabian Peninsula, north to India, and as far west as Spain.

During the 7th century CE, Arab Muslim armies began conquering vast amounts of territory. They managed to take over the Byzantines. It only took twenty years for the Arabs to take over three continents, bringing Muslim rule to a large portion of the Silk Road.

During the Umayyad dynasty, which lasted from 661 to 750 CE, and the Abbasid dynasty, which lasted from 750 to 1250 CE, Islamic and Arabic culture really began to take hold and grow in the newly conquered territories. This was partially because a centralized political state developed. Tribal leaders were replaced by one main monarch, who fully united the territory both politically and religiously. Arabic became the main language, which helped to establish a national identity.

Under the rule of the Abbasid dynasty, the Islamic Golden Age began, which carried on through the 13th century. Religious scholars taught in prestigious institutions, arts flourished, and knowledge spread. There were also many conversions to Islam.

Islamic architecture left a long-lasting impact on the Silk Road that still continues to this day. Remember the domed mosques and minarets we spoke about in the previous chapter? And do not forget about the blue tiles that were influenced by the blue and white porcelain from the Ming dynasty, which led to a legacy of blue-domed mosques all across the world.

Scholars from the Islamic Golden Age also left a lasting impression on the West. For example, we do not typically use Roman numerals to

---

[19] https://en.wikipedia.org/wiki/Islam_in_the_Philippines

write our numbers. We use the Arabic style of writing, which was developed by Islamic scholars and spread westward with trade and cultural exchange.

Many popular works of poetry and literature emerged during this time period. The famous *One Thousand and One Nights*, also often known as *Arabian Nights*, is just one example. This set of stories includes "Aladdin's Wonderful Lamp," "Ali Baba and the Forty Thieves," and "Sinbad the Sailor." These stories have been retold and remastered time and time again throughout history.

Hinduism and Buddhism

Both Hinduism and Buddhism originated in the country of India. They spread in pockets along the Silk Road over hundreds of years and left a legacy of architectural and artistic history.

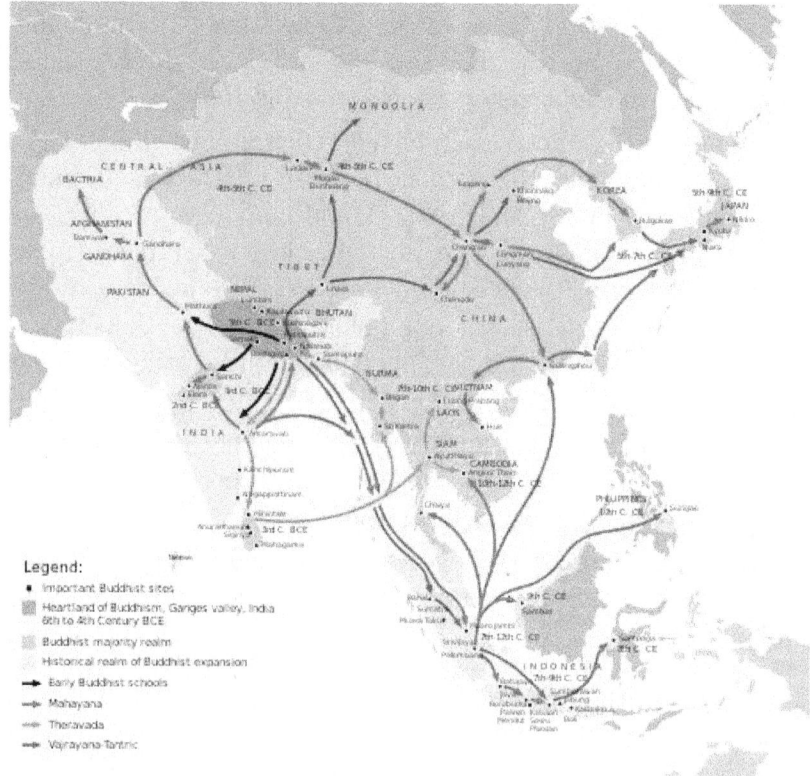

The spread of Buddhism along the Silk Road.
Gunawan Kartapranata, CC BY-SA 3.0 <https://creativecommons.org/licenses/by-sa/3.0>, via Wikimedia Commons; https://commons.wikimedia.org/wiki/File:Buddhist_Expansion.svg

Hinduism was first introduced to China by Indian merchants in the 2nd century CE. Hindu temples sporadically dotted the areas of the Silk Road in China that bordered India; however, all of these temples have been lost to time and weather.

In the previous chapter, we discussed the amazing caves in Xi'an, China, which are filled with a thousand years of Buddhist artwork. Did you know there were also Hindu figures and icons found amidst the statues and art? In addition, many stupas also contain Hindu-influenced statues.

Buddhism was introduced in the 5th century CE. Buddhism began to decline when the Tang dynasty collapsed, and during the 7th century, it was replaced by Islam, which spread along the Silk Road into the port cities on China's southeastern coast in the 7th century CE by Arab merchants. During the 13th century CE, the Mongols brought more Islamic influences deeper into China. Today, there are an estimated eighteen million Muslim adults in China, and there are ten Muslim ethnic groups.[20]

Iconography, an important feature of both Hinduism and Buddhism, was forbidden in Islam, leading to the destruction of many statues and paintings, leaving stupas abandoned to the sun and sand.

When looking back in time, it is clear that Buddhist art left a permanent impact on central Asian art forms. Hellenized Greek art gave the world the first Buddhist statues. Did you know the first Buddha statues resembled the Greek god Apollo?

Greek style permeated Buddhist art, but the foundation for Buddhist architecture remained firmly Indian in nature. The paintings left behind in caves give us countless clues to life during those one thousand years of history. We can see the physical features of the people who traveled to China from various regions, including some who had blonde or red hair. We can see styles of clothing rise in popularity and then disappear, only to be replaced by clothing from a different prominent culture infiltrating the area. The wealth of knowledge contained in Buddhist art is endless.

---

[20] "Islam in China | Pew Research Center."

https://www.pewresearch.org/religion/2023/08/30/islam/#:~:text=Islam%20was%20brought%20to%20China,Islam%20began%20to%20spread%20inland.

A Long-lasting Effect

There is one remaining long-lasting aspect of religion on the Silk Road that we have not yet discussed. That is cosmopolitanism on the Silk Road. If you think about the people who traveled the Silk Road, including missionaries and religious scholars, you must consider that these people set out hoping to meet other humans with viewpoints different than their own.

Part of the adventure and part of the knowledge to be shared and gained involved encountering people from opposing religions and cultures. This is also part of the practice of diplomacy.

Through Silk Road diplomacy, humankind practiced the art of exchanging gifts, learning about others with an open mind, and receiving new information about cultural ideas. Sometimes, this was received with hostility, but other times, it was accepted peacefully.

If we look at the remaining manuscripts we have that were left behind by Silk Road travelers, they all have something important in common. Many of them were distinctly motivated by religion or used religion as the basis of their diplomatic experiences as they traveled and interacted on the trade routes.

Consider Buddhist travelers. Buddhism dictates that a person is always on a spiritual journey, both on Earth and metaphysically, in order to learn and grow as a person. This worldview undoubtedly defined the way Buddhist travelers interacted with travelers who were different from them. This tolerance paved the way for smoother trade and easier connections between cultures on the Silk Road.

People along the Silk Road Today

Today, the political and moral landscape has been forever changed by the Silk Road. The physical paths have long since faded in some areas, but many oasis cities remain. A few of those cities are Khiva, Bukhara, Samarkand, Konye-Urgench, and Almaty.

These cities all have one main thing in common: they are primarily Islamic cities.

The enduring impact of Islam is still felt in Middle Eastern and central Asian cities. Not only are the majority of people Muslim, but the architecture also consists of minarets and domes in the Persian and Islamic styles; it is almost as if time has stood still for thousands of years.

Khiva, Uzbekistan's inner town, known as Itchan Kala, is a UNESCO World Heritage Site. The old city is filled with ornate mosques and tiled minarets and is considered an essential center of the Islamic faith.

Bukhara, Uzbekistan, is a two-thousand-year-old city that also features mosques, tiled minarets, and madrassas. It is home to the 10th-century Muslim architect Samani, and the city is considered the intellectual center of the Islamic world. The city has been impeccably preserved, even remaining the same when Russian influence threatened to take over the region.

Samarkand, Uzbekistan, is considered one of the oldest inhabited cities in central Asia. It has ornate blue-tiled buildings. According to legend, a cousin of the Prophet Muhammad is buried in the city.

Konye-Urgench, Turkmenistan, was a prominent Silk Road trading hub from the 10th to the 14th century. The people living there today still practice Islam.

It is remarkable to think that the Silk Road first came into existence several millennia ago, yet the architectural, religious, and political influences still remain strong today.

Chapter 8: The Silk Road: Science and Technology

Thus far, we have discussed almost every aspect of the Silk Road except for one thing: science and technology. The Silk Road was, of course, home to the exchange of scholarly ideas, and this included scientific advancements. In fact, once people got together to share their ideas and bridge the gaps between different cultures, religions, languages, and locations, history shows that science and technology began to advance rapidly.

Astronomy

One of the first sciences to emerge as an area of study along the Silk Road was astronomy. People used the skies to determine when was the best time to plant or harvest crops, when to host a yearly festival, or to judge the incoming weather. Ancient people combined astronomy and astrology together, thinking they could use the stars to predict the future as well as the seasons.

In 3000 BCE, the Babylonians of Mesopotamia became the first culture on record to begin officially studying these concepts. It turns out the Babylonians worshiped three main celestial gods. Those were the sun, the moon, and the planet Venus.

Their temples were called ziggurats. They looked like pyramids with stairsteps on their sides, which allowed a worshiper to feel closer to the gods in the sky. Their priests did the only logical thing one could think of when worshiping gods in the sky. They carefully watched the movements of the sun, the moon, and Venus until they were able to accurately predict the movements of these heavenly bodies. By 450 BCE, they were able to use mathematics to determine the locations of the sun, the moon, and the planets in the sky.

Shortly before 370 BCE, the trade route appeared on the scene, and the Babylonians' astronomical advances left the region of present-day Sudan with the Greek astronomer and philosopher Democritus. Democritus paid a visit to Babylon, where he learned about the mathematical calculations for the locations of the stars and planets. He then traveled the trade route through Asia Minor and into Egypt, sharing knowledge as he went.[21]

Another Greek philosopher had visited the Babylonians as well. Thales of Miletus, who lived from 640 to 550 BCE, was able to use the Babylonians' mathematical skills to accurately calculate the eclipse of the sun. He combined these skills with Egyptian knowledge to navigate a ship by looking at the stars.

Meanwhile, in India, the astronomy bug was spreading. The Indians displayed both Greek and Babylonian astronomy skills in their own version of astronomy. They translated technical terms from Greek and created their own astrological chart.

Eventually, Indian scholars took both Buddhism and their own astrological knowledge to China along the Silk Road, where China integrated Indian astrological knowledge with their own discoveries. As we speed right along in history, in the 700s, Indian astronomers brought information about the calculation of eclipses and other important related documents based on Greek and Persian discoveries to the caliph's court in Baghdad, where they were translated into Arabic.[22] Astronomy became a major part of the Islamic Golden Age.

We can clearly follow the path of astronomical knowledge back and forth along the trade routes between societies and see how the information grew over time.

Did you know the New Year celebration was determined by ancient astronomical calculations? It is still celebrated every year on March 21st in many Silk Road regions today, including Azerbaijan, India, Iran,

---

[21] https://www.worldhistory.org/Democritus/

[22] https://en.unesco.org/silkroad/sites/default/files/knowledge-bank-article/ways%20of%20scientific%20exchange.pdf

Kyrgyzstan, Pakistan, Turkey, and Uzbekistan.

The New Year celebration is called Nowruz, with variants of the spelling changing slightly based on country and language. Each country and culture has different traditions they celebrate on this day. In Kyrgyzstan, they practice traditional wrestling. In Iran, tales and legends of the mythical King Jamshid are shared with children, and everyone leaps over fires and streams. Other traditions include tightrope walking, horse racing, and leaving lit candles in doorways.

Every region celebrates with song and dance. There are large sacred meals shared among relatives and neighbors. Hard-boiled eggs are decorated in many countries, and there are plenty of activities for children to enjoy.

The main idea behind the New Year celebration is to foster a spirit of community and bridge the gap between local cultures and neighbors. Families reunite, communities come together, and solidarity is promoted between generations.

Mathematics

A close relative of astronomy is mathematics. They go hand in hand, so naturally, math was promoted and shared along the Silk Road.

The Babylonians and Egyptians were some of the earliest pioneers of mathematics, though the subject did not yet have its name. When the Greeks got a hold of the information, their scholars took off and began developing all sorts of calculations.

Our aforementioned Greek philosopher, Thales of Miletus, was also a merchant and a businessman. He realized that math was an important skill to possess when it came to diplomacy and trade. Thales of Miletus was the founder of the mathematical basis that led to Pythagoras's mathematical breakthrough shortly after.

Greek mathematical knowledge traveled along the Silk Road to the Arabs, where the Islamic Golden Age eventually catapulted math to the next level. Funnily enough, the Arabs were very interested in casting their horoscopes, which inspired them to use geometry in astronomical calculations.

The Silk Road carried mathematical knowledge once again with the Muslims into Spain, where the University of Toledo gathered a massive number of mathematical books. Once the Christians reconquered Spain, they raided the university and ended up adopting the Arabic numeral system as their own. Today, we still use Arabic numerals instead of Roman numerals in our math. But here is a little-known secret. The Arabic numerals actually came from India before they were adopted by the Arabs, thanks to the Silk Road information highway.

Alchemy

Around two thousand years ago, humanity began practicing something called alchemy. This English word is derived from the Arabic term *al kimya*.[23] This was the earliest form of chemistry known to humankind.

You may have heard the legends and stories about ancient alchemists who thought they could find the magic formula to change plain metals into precious gold. While this was a laughable pursuit fraught with errant magic, history shows us that these early scientists did begin to develop the scientific method in their experimentation, which set them on the path to making legitimate discoveries.

Meanwhile, the Chinese were in their corner, trying to use alchemy to find the secret of immortality. During this experimentation, the Chinese made a number of accidental discoveries, including gunpowder! Talk about the opposite of immortality, right? Imagine trying to find something that makes humanity live forever and instead discovering the very substance that would go on to kill millions throughout history.

Knowledge from Chinese experiments gradually filtered down the Silk Road toward the west with Indian and Arab traders.

Gunpowder did not reach the Islamic world or Europe until the 13th century. The first known use of gunpowder in the Arab world was in 1326 when Arab soldiers used gunpowder in an attack against the Moors. After that, word began to spread across Europe. Florence ordered the manufacture of cannons and cannonballs shortly after the Islamic battle with the Moors. By the middle of the 14th century, gunpowder had become a regular feature in European warfare.

The real winners in the study of alchemy were the Islamic scientists. Islamic alchemy was taken very seriously. Muslims combined the use of actual science with magic spells. Muslims also received knowledge about alchemy from Hellenistic Greece. During their conquests, Muslims gathered knowledge from the Persians and the Indians.

---

[23] https://www.encyclopedia.com/philosophy-and-religion/other-religious-beliefs-and-general-terms/miscellaneous-religion/alchemy

In the end, Muslims amassed a vast wealth of knowledge on alchemy, which led them to practice actual chemistry. They also began exploring knowledge of mineralogy, which is the study of the Earth's minerals.

Their knowledge continued to spread westward as time went on, reaching Spain through Muslim traders.

Medicine

The study of alchemy and chemistry led to the study of medicine. Medical knowledge as we know it today was rudimentary to nonexistent during the earliest days of the Silk Road. Many cultures believed illness to be the work of evil spirits, malevolent gods, or witchcraft because they had no understanding of germ theory, bacteria, or homeostasis.

Indians wrote the *Sushruta Samhita,* which defines Ayurveda, around 700 BCE. This is India's most renowned ancient medical text. It was quite advanced for the time. The Indians were able to perform surgeries, including the removal of cataracts from the eyes. They seemed to have a thorough grasp of the workings of the digestive system and most other systems within the human body. They realized that disease was caused by an imbalance in the body, and they understood that bad things could be driven out of the body with medicinal plants, in addition to maintaining a good balance of physical and spiritual energy in the body.

The Greeks were not nearly as advanced, and they knew it. Alexander the Great asked Indian doctors to travel with his army, and some of them stayed with the army when the soldiers returned home to Greece, bringing their medical knowledge with them.

The Greeks did have several great medical claims to fame, however. You have probably heard of Hippocrates, who was known as the "Father of Medicine" for his careful recordkeeping. He wrote down both what worked and what did not. His studies were passed on to Muslims after a number of years, contributing to the overall building blocks of all branches of the medical field.

Do you think medicine contributed to diplomacy along the Silk Road? There are several ways medical treatments could have contributed to diplomacy. In those days, herbs were often used as a form of medicine. A region's herbs could be given as a diplomatic gift by travelers to foreign lands. A gift of herbs or medical substances packed a double punch. They were difficult to acquire, and they also showed the gift-giver cared about the well-being of the recipient.

Let us not forget about the big picture, too! Scientific knowledge was shared between cultures along the Silk Road in the ultimate diplomatic exchange. The sharing of advanced ideas was more than diplomacy; it was a collaboration for the advancement of humankind.

The Compass and Other Technological Innovations

The Silk Road facilitated quite a few inventions that have had a long-lasting impact on humanity as a whole.

One of those inventions was the compass. First created by the Chinese during the Han dynasty, the compass was initially made of lodestone. That is an ore of iron with natural magnetization so that it automatically orients itself toward the Earth's poles when it is able to turn freely.

Scholars estimate that the Chinese began using the compass for navigation sometime between the 9th and the 11th century.

Later versions of the compass brought more complexity and some improvements; however, the basic compass was born along the Silk Road in China.

Papermaking, as discussed in a previous chapter, was a major technological innovation that rocked the world. It first spread in popularity within China, where they tried to keep their methods a secret. Later, papermaking spread along the Silk Road to the outer edges of Asia and into Europe.

Paper was used to share knowledge efficiently, allowing cultures to write down their religious beliefs and academic discoveries, making them readily shareable. Information could be reliably passed on consistently without the natural changes that occur when information is shared only by word of mouth in the oral tradition.

Papermaking led to the invention of woodblock printing presses during the Tang dynasty. In an imperial degree in 593 CE, the emperor ordered Buddhist images to be printed.

From there, the Chinese printed on textiles and printed Buddhist texts. They used a woodblock printing method to print short texts that people could wear as charms. Eventually, they began printing longer manuscripts as scrolls, some of which were found in the famous Buddhist caves near the city of Dunhuang.

By the year 1000 CE, scrolls were out of fashion, and books with pages were being printed. By the 11th century, the Chinese had invented movable type and cheaper paper, making books easier to print and more accessible to the common person.

The printing of books further aided the spread of knowledge along the Silk Road. Prior to books, people had to spend time writing out information. The reliable printed book was a game changer for scholars. These books could be shared and passed from one traveler to the next, or they could be amassed in a library for scholars to travel to and read.

Today, the ancient tradition of Chinese block printing is carried on by a handful of dedicated artisans in China. It takes a team of half a dozen people to create woodblock prints. The blocks are made from fine-grained pear or jujube wood cut down to two centimeters thick. They are then sanded smooth until they are fully prepared for engraving.

The desired images are brushed onto extremely thin paper and then transferred onto the blocks, where an engraver carves the images into the thin wood. They are carved in a manner that leaves the images raised, not indented, making a stamp. When the images are finally ready, they are brushed with ink and pressed onto paper by hand.

Some other noteworthy inventions on the Silk Road include glassmaking, metallurgy, dyeing textiles, irrigation, and the creation of paper currency.

The Silk Road's legacy shines through in many areas. The Silk Road laid the foundation for modern-day science principles in chemistry and mathematics, including the invention of algebra. Today, books are a standard commodity around the world.

The globalization brought about by the Silk Road set the stage for an interconnected world, one where we practice diplomacy and trade. It also left a lasting chain of connections all across Asia, Europe, and North Africa that affected many areas of life.

Chapter 9: The Silk Legacy

The Silk Road might have dissolved with the ease of modern travel, but its legacy will forever continue shaping cultures and societies across the world.

Religious Legacy

The spread of religion through the Silk Road has been one of its most powerful legacies. It still impacts our world today. Millions of people were introduced to Christianity, Islam, Buddhism, and Hinduism from their travels on the Silk Road. In turn, they took home these new beliefs to their communities, where those beliefs blended with the local culture.

The first one thousand years of the Common Era saw waves of new religions spread from west to east. Buddhism spread out of India through central Asia and across China, leaving behind the impressive Mogao Caves in Dunhuang, China, which are filled with centuries of Buddhist art and architecture.

Stupas have been uncovered by archaeologists all across the Silk Road. A stupa in Myanmar was excavated and found to match the style of a stupa in Amaravathi, located on the eastern coast of India.

Buddhism blended with Hinduism, as evidenced by amazing artwork inside the Ajanta and Ellora caves in India.

Zoroastrianism brought the Silk Road regions the first idea of a monotheistic god, which spread through the Silk Road and laid the foundation for a moral code and struggle against good and evil. This paved the way for Judaism, Christianity, and Islam.

Tradesmen, merchants, and missionaries helped spread religion and new ideas. This gave rise to the many shared cultural influences linking together places and people all along the Silk Road.

We can look at the present day and find hints of the Silk Road still evident today all over the world, not just in the central Asian and Middle Eastern regions.

Nomadic Legacy

In the United States, though the trade route never ran through those lands, we still can see remnants of the Silk Road in people's daily lives. Americans drink tea out of fine china cups, with that tea coming from tea leaves found around the world. Some Americans regularly visit a mosque. Most of the products invented and traded on the Silk Road are still important to people today, such as paper, ceramics, cotton and silk textiles, metalwork, and even glass.

The wealthy among us purchase fine oriental carpets, and even cheaper knock-off carpets have various patterns emulating Turkish or Persian weaves. Think about the history of carpets across the Silk Road. Nomads moved around with their sheep, weaving distinct carpets with wool fibers in the places where they stopped to rest across ancient Iran and central Asia.

Consider the fine Turkmen carpet weavers who are still making carpets today. Their ancestors fled the persecution of the tsars and resettled in Afghanistan, among other places. After the Taliban persecuted them in Afghanistan, they fled to Pakistan. Their history consists of nomadic travelers along the regions of the Silk Road, and the Turkmens still travel to this day, though under different circumstances. There is one constant in their lives: they weave carpets with the same patterns as their ancestors.

The Tibetans tell a similar story of travel. After fleeing Chinese dominion, they moved into Nepal and India, following the ancient trade routes of their ancestors. Now, they are living in a new place, weaving historical patterns into cloth as if nothing has changed in thousands of years.

In southwestern Iran, the Persian carpet weavers of Fars still practice their ancient craft in the present day. The skills are passed down from generation to generation by oral tradition. Men shear the wool from their sheep in the autumn, and women spin it into yarn. While the yarn is being spun, men build traditional carpet looms that look like a horizontal frame on the ground. Colored yarn is tied to a web of wool to create a carpet.

The women do the weaving. The designs are based on their nomadic lives. No weaver ever creates the same design twice; each one is unique. The colors are created using wool yarn and dye. The Fars people create dye with items collected in nature. The blues, reds, whites, and browns of the carpets are produced from lettuce leaf, pomegranate skin, cherry stem, walnut skin, and indigo.

When the carpet is finished, they sew the sides down and then burn away any extra wool. This leaves vivid designs that are then washed clean and dried before the final product is presented for sale.

Today, nomadic people still live in Eurasia and follow a way of life based on the traditions of the Silk Road. They include Siberian reindeer herders, Mongolian horse breeders, Tibetan yak herders, and Turkmen shepherds.

These nomadic people were responsible for significant Silk Road contributions beyond just weaving and carpets. They introduced felted wool to the world, which they used to keep warm and dry. They invented harnesses for horses and livestock, created unique bowed string instruments, and developed sustainable portable housing called yurts.

The Legacy of Silk and Fashion

Silk was, naturally, the most well-known product of the Silk Road. The Roman obsession with silk vaulted it into luxury item status. Wherever silk went, money and creativity followed. We can witness the same treatment of high fashion items today, some of which are still made from silk.

Today, China has the International Silk Festival to celebrate the fashion and cultivation of silk. This festival includes a themed fashion show. For example, in 2016, the International Silk Festival's fashion show had a theme of four earth elements on what they called High Fashion Night. They featured Exquisite Metal, Charming Wood, Merged Water and Fire, and Comprehensive Element Earth. The show released twenty-eight fashion trends for the 2017 season.

India also has an international silk fair every year, during which vendors from around the world come to sell silk products in one large trade show with up to 150 merchants.

Like the days of the Silk Road, fashion is often divisive and creative. Fashion designers from Japan and central Asia still incorporate silk into their intricate designs. In India, Uzbekistan, and Syria, embroidery is still being sewed by hand onto silk garments.

In China, the silkworm plays a major role in some regions. Local traditions include the Silkworm Flower Festival, which began in 2014 as a revival of the Silk Road's silk heritage. It takes place yearly in the southern Chinese town of Zhenze, which is known as the hometown of the silkworm. The yearly festival is meant to showcase the current silkworm industry and boost tourism in the area.

The local farmers believe the goddess of silkworms is in charge of the silk harvest, and sacrifices are made to her at the festival. Female silkworm farmers dress beautifully with silk and paper flowers. They make harvest offerings to the goddess as part of the festival.

Gastronomic Legacy

Food cooked today in Silk Road regions is considered another part of the cultural heritage of the Silk Road. Today, along the trade routes, each culture has its own unique flavors and traditions, yet somehow, all of the places still retain links to each other left over from thousands of years of interconnected trade.

In Iran, you will find freshly cooked flatbreads being sold at markets from wooden carts. The breads are flavored with familiar herbs and spices, such as onion, garlic, sesame, and cumin. Travel along the old trade routes to India, Pakistan, Afghanistan, and other parts of central Asia, and what will you find? The same flatbread with different local names and different spices added to it, giving each region a unique flavor.

Familiar fruits and vegetables fill market stalls in these countries as well. You will find fresh persimmons, pomegranates, figs, peaches, grapes, leeks, ginger, and onions. Each region makes slightly different recipes with the same main ingredients.

Another common culinary bond between regions of the Silk Road is the love for dumplings or bread with fillings. China has the mantou, Japan refers to this sweetened filled bread as manju, and in Korea, it is mandu, which is a ravioli-type dumpling filled with beef. Tibetans have filled dumplings called momo. Turkey, Armenia, and Iran have wonton-style pasta with meat, cheese, and/or vegetables as well.

Musical Legacy

Music on the Silk Road has had a major impact on cultures. The world's music is astonishingly diverse, though the most foundational instruments are similar. The human voice, instruments made from natural wood with strings added, flute-style instruments that produce sounds by blowing, and drum-style instruments that produce sound by banging on a hollow object are the most common.

The use of music is similar across all cultures as well, being used for both pleasure and as a part of traditions.

How did music on the Silk Road spread and change over time?

The people on the Silk Road can characteristically be divided into two separate groups: nomads and sedentary peoples. One thing both groups have in common, even if there were multiple conflicts between them, is their music.

When travelers journeyed along the Silk Road, they might have hosted some of the world's first international jam sessions. Imagine nighttime around a fire in a remote Hindu Kush valley or in a cold, desolate desert. Music was a welcome distraction for weary travelers, providing both entertainment and comfort.

Many instruments played by nomadic people along the Silk Road reached Europe rather quickly. This includes lutes, oboes, drums, and zithers. The first violin was likely based on a Mongolian instrument made with horsehair strings. This instrument was held upright and played with horsehair bows. The scroll at the top of the modern morin khuur stringed instrument today is a carved horse's head based on the original Mongol version.

The history of the fiddle can be traced through East Asia and seen in the kamancheh instrument. Indonesia undoubtedly experienced the stringed instrument during the spice trade, fashioning their own version called the rebab.

Nomadic people had a tradition of the bard, a musician who recited poetry or sang in a storytelling style accompanied by music they made themselves, such as a drum beat to represent horse hooves. In communities that are now sedentary, the musical style of the bard still persists today, revealing clues about their nomadic ancestry.

Other musical ties bound the different religions and cultures along the Silk Road, and these are still clearly present in cultural music today.

For example, the Buddhists introduced monastic chanting to the world. Present-day Christian Assyrian choirs still sing in monastic chanting, matching the same style of scales and melodic modes of the Middle Eastern Islamic world. Armenia, which is home to one of the Middle East's oldest Christian cultures, and Jewish cantillation both display similar styles of chanting and modal tones.

Today, the music of the Silk Road is still being made. However, the people are far more scattered. Music of the Silk Road remains a link between communities, especially those that have been scattered by immigration or wars. Afghan musicians compose new songs even though they may be living in New York City, Toronto, or Peshawar. Bukharan Jewish music has almost been eradicated from Bukhara, but it is alive and well within expatriate communities in Tel Aviv and New York.

Today, the Aga Khan Music Programme in central Asia collaborates with the Smithsonian Institute and the Silk Road Project to keep the musical traditions of the central Asian portion of the Silk Road alive and thriving in the face of wars, famine, and political upheaval. They currently have projects in Kazakhstan, Kyrgyzstan, Tajikistan, Uzbekistan, and Afghanistan.

Famous cellist Yo-Yo Ma is a well-spoken artist who promotes musical and cultural exchange between present-day Silk Road regions. Born in Paris to Chinese parents before immigrating to the US as a child, Yo-Yo Ma has experienced his fair share of migration. His father was a violinist who focused on bridging the gap between China and the West with music.

Yo-Yo Ma summed up the present-day preservation of Silk Road cultures perfectly when he said, "As a crucible for cultural intermingling, the lands of the Silk Road, then and now, offer an unparalleled vantage point from which to understand vitally alive and ever-evolving languages of music, art, and craft that may seem by turns familiar and exotic. Our challenge is to embrace the wondrous diversity of artistic expression while remaining mindful of the common humanity that links us all."[24]

Today, work is being done by organizations like UNESCO to preserve the intangible cultural heritage of the Silk Road. UNESCO stands for the United Nations Educational, Scientific and Cultural

---

[24] "A Journey of Discovery | Smithsonian Folklife Festival"
https://festival.si.edu/2002/the-silk-road/a-journey-of-discovery/smithsonian

Organization. Their goal is to "promote knowledge sharing and the free flow of ideas to accelerate mutual understanding and a more perfect knowledge of each other's lives."[25]

They define intangible cultural heritage as "traditions or living expressions inherited from our ancestors and passed on to our descendants, such as oral traditions, performing arts, social practices, rituals, festive events, knowledge and practices concerning nature and the universe or the knowledge and skills to produce traditional crafts."[26]

UNESCO works to provide in-depth and culturally relevant information on different subjects related to the Silk Road to promote understanding and keep traditions alive. It is a fabulous resource for all things related to the Silk Road.

While we have collections of artifacts that survived the years and give us fascinating clues to study about life during the time of the Silk Road, the real jewels are the intangible cultural heritage still present today in descendants of people who lived along the Silk Road. However, as our world becomes increasingly globalized, these pockets of traditional cultures are at risk of being lost forever.

The Belt and Road Initiative

Did you know there is a collective effort to bring back the Silk Road?

China is working to revive the Silk Road as a new initiative known as the Belt and Road Initiative (BRI). Its goal is to enhance connectivity through trade, boost economies, and grow diplomacy through Asia, Europe, and Africa.

The BRI was first announced by China's president, Xi Jinping, in 2013. The inspiration and name were based on the original Silk Road trade routes. Similar to the original Silk Road, the intentions are to foster connections and exchange cultural information along with trade.

What does Belt and Road mean? The two main components of the BRI are the "Silk Road Economic Belt" and the "21st Century Maritime Silk Road." The Belt portion will focus on the overland routes connecting China to Europe through central Asia and the Middle East, similar to the original Silk Road's overland routes. The maritime routes

---

[25] "UNESCO in Brief." https://www.unesco.org/en/brief.

[26] "Intangible Cultural Heritage." https://en.unesco.org/silkroad/silk-road-themes/intangible-cultural-heritage.

will connect China to Southeast Asia, Africa, and Europe.

In order to pull off the BRI, a large amount of infrastructure has to be developed, and countries must cooperate with each other to sync up in trade. On the list of infrastructure to be developed are roads, railways, ports, airports, and even pipelines. Energy infrastructure will also need to be in place to power the boats, trains, and trucks traveling along the BRI.

Funding for the BRI is coming from Chinese state-owned enterprises, companies, banks, and other institutions. Foreign investors have started joining in as more countries decide to join the BRI. China even established a new bank to support the project. It is called the Asian Infrastructure Investment Bank (AIIB), and it is linked to something called the Silk Road Fund.

The BRI has already gathered investors and interest from countries in Asia, Europe, Africa, and even Latin America. Recent projects include the China-Pakistan Economic Corridor (CPEC), China-Laos Railway, and the Addis Ababa-Djibouti Railway.

Some countries have worried about political instability caused by the BRI. Will China gain influence and soft power over countries where it promotes trade routes? Looking back at China's history in the original Silk Road, we may be able to guess the answer to that question.

As of recently, the BRI is still expanding. It now includes digital trade initiatives. When people began to worry about the impact of all of the new infrastructure on the ecosystem, China added a green initiative to the BRI.

China would like to add the BRI to the United Nations Sustainable Development Goals. Countries around the world are watching the beginnings of the BRI, and the debate over the pros and cons continues.

Conclusion

The Silk Road was a vast network of trade routes that connected the Far East to the West in the ancient world. It spanned a distance of nearly four thousand miles (over six thousand kilometers) of territory in its entirety.

The origins of the Silk Road began in ancient China around the 2nd century BCE during the Han dynasty. As the centuries went by, the Silk Road witnessed the rise and fall of empires as it expanded and grew. Eventually, the Silk Road extended as far west as the Mediterranean Sea, incorporating trade with the Greeks, Romans, and many other civilizations.

This trade route brought commerce to remote valleys and crossed dangerous deserts and mountains. The Silk Road was also a maritime route later in its history, fostering the iconic spice trade through the oceans and across the globe.

The sea routes began to take preference over the long, treacherous overland routes as navigation technology improved. The sea routes allowed goods to be transported faster and in larger quantities. Maritime markets also increased access to remote locations and allowed isolated societies to participate in trade.

Maritime routes also allowed for direct trips from port to port, giving rise to port cities all along the waterways. These port cities became melting pots of cultures where scholars and religious leaders met with each other to exchange knowledge and ideas. The societies at these ports were greatly enriched by the diverse cultures in their cities.

Maritime trade routes really increased the speed of globalization by connecting the world efficiently and spreading ideas and religion even further than the land routes had done.

We have seen what an impact the Silk Road had on world history. Take a moment and imagine what the world today would be like if the Silk Road had never even existed. Imagine, way back during the Han dynasty, if the emperor had not felt motivated enough to send out a diplomat to explore nearby regions and establish friendly trade.

What all would have been impacted?

Primarily, we can be certain that the world would have developed new ideas at a much slower pace. For example, ideas and technology that made their way to Europe from the Silk Road would have had to find their way abroad by chance rather than by being carried swiftly along with trade goods on a regular basis.

How long would it have taken for the discovery of gunpowder to make its way to the West? After the Europeans were given information about gunpowder, they rushed to develop firearms. This would never have happened without the Silk Road. How would that have had an effect on the success or failure of subsequent wars? How would that have impacted the expansion of territory or the acquisition of natural resources? And how would that have impacted civilians caught in the midst of warfare?

Christopher Columbus discovered some of the islands in the Caribbean while searching for a maritime route to engage in the spice trade. If there was not a Silk Road, would the rush to discover spices have ever occurred? How long would it have taken for the Americas to be discovered and settled by Europeans?

Imagine the long-lasting impact of that. What would the Americas look like today if they had not been discovered by outsiders at that point in time? More than likely, there would be more native peoples in the Americas today. The landscape of the world would also look like a very different place.

Chances are the continents would have been eventually discovered by sailors from Europe at some point in time, but it could have been hundreds or even thousands of years into the future. Medicine may have developed to the point where Europeans could aid native communities suffering from European diseases like smallpox. However, it is hard to know for sure in this hypothetical universe where the Silk Road never existed.

Human migration would have slowed to a halt, leaving communities more isolated from each other. Without the sharing of ideas through trade, communities would have stayed more homogenous, with cultures and religions staying stagnant due to the lack of influence of other people groups.

Think about the Black Death. This horrific disease spread from trade with the Far East into European cities, where it wiped out large amounts of the population. In some cities, more than half of the population died from the plague. Without trade on the Silk Road, diseases like the bubonic plague would have never spread across Europe. Chances are something else may have wiped out the population in place of the plague, but it possibly might not have done so on the same disastrous scale as the plague.

Europe would have lacked many goods and food items that have become commonplace. Imagine the British people without a cuppa tea! We could write an entire book alone on the importance of tea in British culture throughout history.

The Silk Road also contributed to the loss of indigenous beliefs from nomadic and isolated cultures. Without the spread of religion along the Silk Road, these isolated peoples would have held onto their native beliefs for a longer period of time.

Religion on the Silk Road heavily impacted architecture and art, blending cultures and religions together to create all types of unique buildings and artwork. For example, remember the spread of the blue-tiled mosques with minarets across central Asia? This would not have happened without interconnected travel on the trade routes. Art and architecture would have been isolated to their own regions instead of being influenced by other places.

Missionaries would not have been able to travel from place to place as easily since the Silk Road was heavily used as a missionary route. This would have greatly impacted Christianity, which was spread in large numbers by traveling missionaries.

Without a doubt, the Silk Road was the catalyst that caused economic success in many regions, raising empires to great heights and, in turn, leading to their demise when wars and disasters ended or changed trade patterns.

Think of the Roman Empire without silk. What would the Romans have spent their money on if they had not funneled so much of it into China? The absence of luxurious silk would have led to an obsession with a different luxury good that was more local to Rome. What might it have been?

The Romans' style would certainly have been different as well. Without silk, the elite would have had to dress in ordinary wool and linen. Without silk, would the Romans have concentrated on developing their own fancy textiles? While the people of the empire loved silk, they still would have traded other goods and flourished without it. They just may have looked less suave while doing so!

Aside from all of the obvious things we would miss without the trade of goods on the Silk Road, perhaps the largest impact would have been the lack of globalization and diplomacy between cultures.

Without globalization, the world would lack economic growth. People would have no access to a wide range of goods from outside of their home regions. Countries would strive to be economically independent without trade, localizing their industries and focusing on producing goods that lay in their backyards rather than sourcing materials from all around the world, similar to the way nomads weave carpets from resources close to home.

The greatest gift of the Silk Road is the human connection it fostered between unique groups of people. The richness and depth humanity as a whole has gained from the sharing of music, art, food, and knowledge can never be replicated.

The Silk Road represents the human spirit of adventure, showing the unending desire we possess to connect with others across vast distances and over challenging terrain. The Silk Road shows how determined humans are to find prosperity, even in the face of dangerous sea voyages or when faced with the steep Hindu Kush mountain range.

Without the unbreakable threads linking civilizations along the Silk Road, we would be isolated, likely remaining in hostile pockets of civilization and lacking the most wonderful parts of what it means to enjoy life to the fullest: the shared connections between people.

Here's another book by Enthralling History that you might like

Free limited time bonus

Stop for a moment. We have a free bonus set up for you. The problem is this: we forget 90% of everything that we read after 7 days. Crazy fact, right? Here's the solution: we've created a printable, 1-page pdf summary for this book that you're reading now. All you have to do to get your free pdf summary is to go to the following website:

https://livetolearn.lpages.co/enthrallinghistory/

Once you do, it will be intuitive. Enjoy, and thank you!

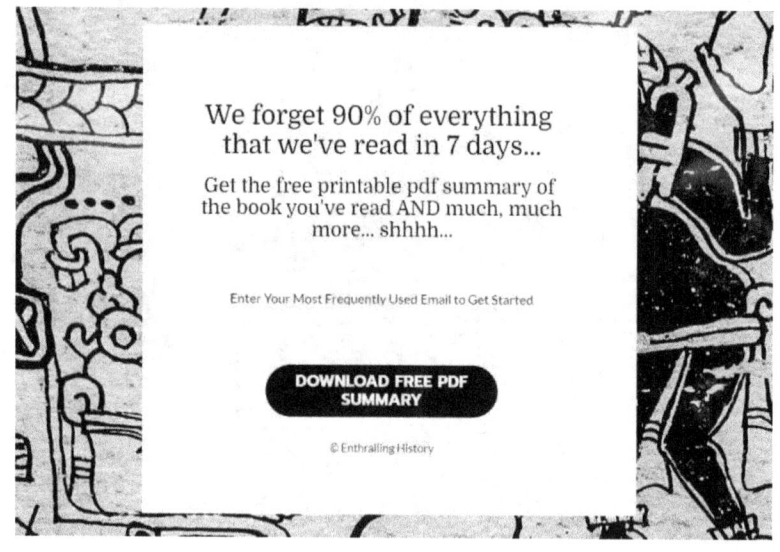

Bibliography

Christian, David. "Silk Roads or Steppe Roads?" https://www.jstor.org/stable/20078816.

Torr, Geordie. *The Silk Roads: A History of the Great Trading Routes Between East and West.*

"Ancient Tea and Horse Caravan Road." http://www.silkroadfoundation.org/newsletter/2004vol2num1/tea.htm.

"Ancient Tea Horse Road." https://www.bbc.com/travel/article/20120830-asias-ancient-tea-horse-road.

Fan Ye. *Hou Hanshu* (*Book of the Later Han*).

"Trade under the Tang Dynasty." https://courses.lumenlearning.com/suny-hccc-worldcivilization/chapter/trade-under-the-tang-dynasty/.

"The Prosperity of the Silk Road in the Tang Dynasty." http://en.shaanxi.gov.cn/as/hac/hos/201704/t20170428_1595517.html.

"Silk Road Overland Transportation." http://www.historyshistories.com/silk-road-transportation-overland-route.html.

"Transportation Along the Silk Road." http://www.silkroadtourcn.com/blog/160.html.

"Caravans." https://factsanddetails.com/china/cat2/sub90/item1103.html.

"Slave Trade on the Silk Road." https://shanghai.nyu.edu/news/exploring-silk-road-slave-trade-turfan.

Herodotus. *Histories.*

"Ibn Battuta." https://www.khanacademy.org/humanities/big-history-project/expansion-interconnection/exploration-interconnection/a/ibn-battuta.

"Palmyra." https://en.unesco.org/silkroad/content/palmyra.

"Cosmopolitan Silk Road." https://academic.oup.com/isagsq/article/2/1/ksac007/6556077.

"A Journey of Discovery | Smithsonian Folklife Festival." https://festival.si.edu/2002/the-silk-road/a-journey-of-discovery/smithsonian.

"Intangible Cultural Heritage." https://en.unesco.org/silkroad/silk-road-themes/intangible-cultural-heritage.

"Discovering the Islamic architecture of the Silk Road - Saga." https://www.saga.co.uk/magazine/travel/destinations/asia/central-asia/silk-road-islamic-architecture

"CHRISTIANITY, NESTORIANS AND THE SILK ROAD" https://factsanddetails.com/china/cat2/sub90/entry-8324.html

"How Islam got to the Philippines." https://slate.com/news-and-politics/2005/01/how-islam-got-to-the-philippines.html

"Islam in the Philippines - Wikipedia." https://en.wikipedia.org/wiki/Islam_in_the_Philippines

"Islam in China | Pew Research Center." https://www.pewresearch.org/religion/2023/08/30/islam/#:~:text=Islam%20was%20brought%20to%20China,Islam%20began%20to%20spread%20inland.

"Democritus - World History Encyclopedia." https://www.worldhistory.org/Democritus/.

"Alchemy | Encyclopedia.com." https://www.encyclopedia.com/philosophy-and-religion/other-religious-beliefs-and-general-terms/miscellaneous-religion/alchemy.

"Inventions and Trade: The Silk and Spice Routes, 1994." https://en.unesco.org/silkroad/sites/default/files/knowledge-bank-article/ways%20of%20scientific%20exchange.pdf.

"UNESCO in Brief." https://www.unesco.org/en/brief

www.ingramcontent.com/pod-product-compliance
Lightning Source LLC
Chambersburg PA
CBHW070341010526
44107CB00004B/577